Reflections on Murky Water

My Vietnam Chronicle

By
Louis Remmers

Printed in the U.S.A. by
SprintPrint
114 North Spring Street
Tupelo, Mississippi 38804

ISBN 978-0-9894957-1-4

For
My wife, Linda
My daughters, Kimberly and Stacy,
and family

Every day is a gift!
Live, love & laugh!
love Clemmens

A very special thanks to Mrs. Janie Alexander-Macaso for her tireless dedication to this project. Without her help, it would not have been possible.

Contents

Foreword

Coming of age in America in the 1960s was intense. The flames of war were burning brightly in faraway Vietnam; in the deep South and my growing up in Mississippi, deep racism was being challenged by a civil rights army fighting for change, the flames of war all around us. It was a wild and crazy time.

In my senior year of college, Nixon ended college deferments and instituted a lottery, the first since 1942. My number, 27, was a guaranteed February 1970 call up date. What to do? The National Guard and Reserve units were full. Canada was no option, nor was accepting a commission. Finally, signing up for a third year made me a volunteer, letting me avoid the draft, finish college and choose a specialty. So it was in the army's psychiatric hospitals – in Texas and Germany – I labored, working among those caught up in war's collateral damages.

Lou, a Pennsylvania-born, New Jersey-raised boy, grew up in a large, patriotic, working-class, Catholic family. Always tender-hearted, he was bright, dyslexic, and talented, with a goofy sense of humor. Physically tough and strong, he went to work for the Pennsylvania phone company out of high school. Doing well there, it didn't matter, nine months later he was being drafted into the army. Figuring Vietnam would be safer on a boat, he joined the navy. Surely the extra two years would be worth it.

Assigned to the Seabees, in 1966 he headed to Gulfport, Mississippi, where his training began. First was electrician's school, then the rigorous deep-water diving school.

Training done, straight to Vietnam he went. Stationed in Seabee units, his first tour was with Marines on the front lines of battle. Here it was, as his stories tell, the hell of war close up and personal. His second tour ending in October 1969, he flew back to Gulfport just three days after Hurricane Camille had devastated the Mississippi Gulf Coast. With no place for the returnees to stay, in two short weeks they were processed, discharged, and dumped back into civilian life.

Returning to the "real world" was for many war-dazed, changed, and damaged veterans its own particular kind of hell. Home seemed a foreign land. The nation was torn apart by this war. The harsh, strident call of protesters was swelling, growing louder and uglier. Our soldiers were not returning as heroes; too often they were seen as criminals, sometimes called "baby-killers."

Back to New Jersey, it wasn't home anymore. The University of Delaware rejected his application for admission. Trade school wasn't right. Back to Mississippi, then back north, back and forth . . . until marrying Linda. Mississippi then became home. Struggling still, unhappily enrolled at the University of Southern Mississippi, someone suggested a vocational aptitude test, and Lou blew the top off the physical therapy scale. Finally, he had found his calling and life's work.

In God's good, often bent and twisted way, Lou has been blessed to be given such rich fertilizer throughout life. All of it shaping and forming him into the person of deep compassion, integrity, into the healer that he is. His "magic" hands have blessed and healed many of our bodies from the insults and injuries of life while his loving spirit touches us as well. These gathered stories are part of Lou's own healing work, for the scars and damages from war always wound one's soul.

Here in 2013, compassion and healing are still needed for many Vietnam vets. At the same time, growing numbers of war-dazed, changed, and damaged vets have returned from Iraq and are still coming from Afghanistan, many having served multiple tours of duty.

To help all of us remember the incredible toll of war, there is a growing movement to build a smaller version of the Vietnam Wall in Tupelo, Mississippi. One hundred percent of all profits from this book are being given toward the Wall's construction.

Dare we dream and pray and work toward that day when war – and racism – will be no more?

Easter, 2013
Wil Howie
Minister, St. Andrew Presbytery, Presbyterian Church (USA)
Executive Director, Living Waters for the World
Member, Veterans for Peace, Inc.

Lou at Graduation from Boot Camp in Illinois

I'm in the Navy Now

At 7:00 p.m. on a Friday night in June 1965, I was preparing to graduate from Riverside High School. Since I wasn't focused on academics, I wasn't bound for college. The following Monday I was beginning my career with Bell Telephone Company in Philadelphia, Pennsylvania. I had been encouraged to get the job by a phone company executive, the father of a former girlfriend. Although I was a little apprehensive, I was looking forward to not being responsible for homework.

When Monday came, I traveled to Philadelphia by bus and subway to begin my new job making phone connections to the switching equipment at a central office. This would connect phones to dial tones and ultimately tie every phone in the area to a nationwide network.

On this job, I worked rotating shifts, first day, then evenings, and then the graveyard shift. The graveyard shift gave me an opportunity to see the sun come up on my ride home.

I worked hard trying to prove my worth and thought I was in high cotton with take home pay of eighty-six dollars a week. I gave my mother twenty-five dollars each week for room and board, which I realized was free when I was going to school. I spent about ten dollars a week for transportation and another ten for food and Cokes. Most of the remainder I tried to save.

One morning, the office manager came by my workstation to encourage me to keep up the fine work and inform me that my effort to do a good job had been noticed. I would be considered for the next promotion. That news was so exciting that I could hardly wait to get home and tell my parents.

When I arrived home with my good news, my mother had a concerned look on her face as she handed me a large brown envelope. The enclosed letter began, "Greetings from the President of the United States," and continued, "You are hereby directed to report to Newark, New Jersey, for your draft physical for possible induction into the Armed Forces of the United States." The date and time for the physical were given.

The excitement about the job and promotion quickly vanished. My heart sank. Scenes from the war in Vietnam were on the television in our living room every night, and now there was no way I could escape being a part of that escalating conflict.

I had been working with the phone company for about nine months and was going steady with a girl in the community. Vietnam was not in our plans.

Since my father had been in the Navy, I decided to take a day off from work to visit a Navy recruiter. Being drafted meant being a foot soldier in the Army, and I was sure that it would be much safer on a naval ship at sea. The recruiter sold me on a four-year deal with a one-hundred-twenty-day delay before I would have to report. I signed on the dotted line for four years in the Navy instead of two years in the Army. After all, it wouldn't be nearly as dangerous.

The delay days flew by quickly. One morning I woke up as usual with Mother cooking my typical breakfast of four eggs, bacon, and toast, but this day was to be very different. After breakfast, my father drove me to the train station in Philadelphia, Pennsylvania, where I met other young recruits and boarded an old, uncomfortable train to Chicago.

The train ride lasted for almost thirty hours, but we were like school kids on a field trip, soon becoming friends. Telling jokes and stories made the time go by as fast as the clacking of the rails. I played one game of poker, but soon realized I was in over my head with more seasoned young men, so I bowed out with only five dollars fifty cents in hard cash left in my pocket.

When we arrived in Chicago, we began to look around like a bunch of country bumpkins. Before any of us could escape and explore the city, one of the young men, who had been selected in Philadelphia to keep us under control, directed us to a train on another platform. This train had two levels with observation windows and much nicer accommodations.

After we had ridden several miles south, the train stopped in front of a large stone wall. A uniformed gentleman got on and told us to get off and line up in the street next to the train. The man seemed nice, but none of us knew who he was. Was he an officer? Our guide? Possibly, a counselor?

We gingerly walked across the street and through a gate in the wall. We halted our file, and the gates of the Great Lakes Naval Station closed behind us with a big bang. Suddenly our new found friend began yelling at us and wasn't nearly as nice as he had appeared on the train.

We were all given navy blue caps and marched to a barber shop where our heads were shaved. We were then escorted via yelling to a large room where we took the Oath of Allegiance to the Constitution of the United States. After this we were taken to a small building with bunk beds and a tiny shower area and told to get some rest. We were instructed not to keep any radios since we were not to be bothered by the outside world. Did I volunteer for this?

The next morning we were taken to a large, old building and into a room filled with tables on which there were boxes. We were told to strip down to our underwear and put all of our clothes in the boxes, and then put our home addresses on the boxes. When we had finished this task, the boxes were all taken away.

While standing there in our underwear, we were given a sheet of paper on which was written the sizes of our new uniforms and shoes. We were told to get in line and hold the paper in our mouth for safekeeping. Each of us was given a mattress cover, which we were to use as a large bag to collect our new belongings. We dragged the bags between our legs as we continued filing from one room to another.

One of the first rooms we entered had long tables with men standing on them. A man on a table would shout out our sizes, and runners would gather the appropriate sized items and hand them to him. Then he would throw the items of clothing at the recruit for whom they were intended. Items would bounce off the chest and into the bag. This was especially uncomfortable during the shoe toss.

When the bags were full of the new clothing, we were directed to a small room filled with cubicles. In each cubicle were jars of black and white paint and small brushes. Each recruit was given a set of stencils with his name and serial number and instructed at a rapid fire pace to get each item of clothing and stencil our information in the correct place on each piece. After our clothing was labeled, we were permitted to dress in one set. We were now official and all looked the same: scared, sheared, and tired.

The days passed slowly, and we began to change. Our routine was up at 3:00 a.m. to get ready for the long day which ended about 10:00 p.m. Classes were attended. Physical challenges were met. Shots were received. We were shuffled around like cattle. Rain, sleet, or snow did not speed up or slow down our marching from one area to another.

Early one morning as we neared the end of our training, we were marched into a room filled with cubicles that were about eight feet by eight feet. Inside each cubicle was a man sitting behind a small desk and holding a big book. We each went into a cubicle where we were asked what kind of job we wanted in the Navy. None of us had a clue. We were just trying to survive and not think about what the future might hold.

When the man asked me what I did in civilian life, I told him I had worked for the telephone company in Philadelphia, Pennsylvania. He turned to a very large book and after flipping pages said, "How about construction electrician?" I didn't know what that was, and he was not in the proper humor to let me know, so I just said "Okay, I guess." I was in a state of shock, and he had a quota of jobs to fill.

I'm in the Navy, and I have a job. I'm a construction electrician.

Boot Camp Graduation in Illinois

Rhode Island

I did not know what I had gotten into until I arrived in Davisville, Rhode Island, the original home of the U. S. Navy Seabees, to attend construction electrician A school. It was then that I realized I was being taught how to run electrical lines on telephone poles while being shot at.

Upon arrival, I was assigned to a large barracks that had been left over from World War II. All of us shared a very large room and were treated like recruits. If we were seen with idle time, we were given tasks like painting or polishing fire extinguishers.

The winter in Rhode Island that year was very cold, and there was lots of snow, so we were able to transform the fire extinguisher boxes on the outside of the barracks into convenient beer coolers. We could go out on the fire escape and open the small box on the side of the building and get a very cold beer. Although it was totally illegal, we enjoyed it anyway.

After a few weeks, we were reassigned to new buildings that were pastel in color. The facilities were much more modern and were appreciated by all.

We were being trained for a large mix of jobs, such as construction mechanics, equipment operators, builders, electricians, and plumbers. The electrician school consisted of interior wiring, power distribution, electrical theory, physics, and pole climbing.

There was a forest of poles spaced about ten feet apart that we climbed up and down for days. We played catch with a large ball as we threw the ball from one pole to the next, learning how to stretch and maneuver in our climbing gear. We were taught how to manually bore holes in the poles to hang cross arms and string wire.

During the day, we all went to our respective school, and in the evening, we would end up in the barracks with nothing to do. There were various activities on the base, but most of us had little interest in participating.

****

The Davisville Seabee installation was located adjacent to Naval Air Station Quonset Point. One of the main activities that did seem to draw interest was traveling across base to the air station where there was an Enlisted Men's club. There we could have a few cold beers and listen to some music.

As it turned out, the Navy fliers and Seabees did not get along very well and frequent fights broke out. On one occasion a very large group of sailors engaged in a brawl. The EM club was nearly totaled, and after the club was repaired, the commanding officer of the base made it off limits to all Seabees.

The planes at the naval air station were primarily anti-submarine warfare planes that flew along the Atlantic coast, but there were a few other types of planes. I was very interested in getting a closer look.

One day I jumped over the low fence that separated the air station from our Seabee base. I walked to a large plane hangar and looked around at the various aircraft. I had on my normal Navy issue blue work uniform so I blended in.

I climbed in and out of planes, just like a tourist. As I was climbing out of a jet, an officer came walking up. He was a full colonel so I saluted and quickly picked up a clip board that was nearby.

The officer asked me if his plane would be ready for flight the next day. I confirmed that it indeed would be finished and would fly like a new one. He seemed very pleased, and since I had a clip board in hand, I appeared to be official.

I decided that I had seen enough aircraft and quickly made an exit to jump the fence back to the Seabee base. I never turned back and never knew if anyone got chewed out for not having the colonel's plane ready for flight the next day.

****

Those of us who were in the military during the Vietnam War Era had many ways to count the days until we would be discharged and return to the life we had left behind. While I was in Rhode Island, there was a young man in our class who had a very unusual way of clicking off the time he had left to serve.

This man seemed older than the rest of us and extremely vocal about getting out of the Navy. He was very short in stature and his uniform was much more worn than the rest of the class, but he derived a way to count weeks in a very visual way.

He had a small ball chain attached to his belt loop on the right side. The chain hung down, and the end was neatly tucked into his right front pocket much like a chain for a pocket watch is worn. The ball chain was from an old rubber bathtub stopper like those used in the 1940's and 50's to attach the stopper to a vent on the inside of the tub. This man's chain was stainless steel and very shiny. He told us that it was his "short chain." Each week he would cut off one of the balls from the chain to signify that he was one week closer to getting out of the Navy.

When we finished school and his ball chain was much shorter, I'm very sure that he re-enlisted when none of us were looking.

****

Since my family had moved to Delaware while I was in boot camp in Illinois, I calculated that I could go home from Rhode Island to Delaware for weekend visits. Each Wednesday, I began placing fliers on cars with tags from New Jersey, Delaware, or Maryland in hopes of getting a ride south. Several times, I was able to catch a ride by sharing gas money and was able to visit my family if only for a day.

On one occasion, I caught a ride with three other young

men who were heading south. We were in an old worn-out Chevrolet that had a small, six-cylinder engine. Somewhere on the Jersey Turnpike, we were cruising about ninety-miles-an-hour when the engine blew. Fragments of the engine came flying up under my feet through the rusted back seat floorboard. We coasted to a stop and got out of the car.

The owner of the car removed the car tag and said, "Good-bye." We were all forced to hitchhike or walk. I arrived in Delaware around six o'clock in the morning, slept most of the day Saturday, and left Sunday for a bus trip back to Rhode Island. The time may have been short, but the hours spent at home were precious.

After about eight weeks of intense training in Rhode Island, I was shipped off to Gulfport, Mississippi.

Entrance to the Base at Gulfport

Entering Gulfport

Arrival at Gulfport

I arrived in Gulfport, Mississippi in November 1966 after completing boot camp in Chicago and electrician school in Rhode Island. I had taken a commercial flight from Philadelphia, Pennsylvania to Atlanta, Georgia and then to Gulfport. The temperature when I left Philadelphia was seventeen degrees, and when I got to Mississippi, it was in the mid-eighties. I was sure we must have landed in Cuba by mistake.

I caught a taxi to the base, checked in, and was assigned to a barracks at the west end. This base had been closed since the end of World War II and was very rundown. The barracks, long buildings with windows open to the world on each side, had showers at the end but no hot water or water fountains. Open light bulbs hanging from wires in the ceiling provided the only lighting.

The wooden floors had long since dried out, causing them to be filled with splinters as large as your thumb. This made it necessary for us to walk around with our boots on since the splinters were just waiting to catch shower shoes and shred them.

The base had an Enlisted Men's' Club that was housed in an old garage and furnished with two picnic tables and a few coolers of beer. The base dining facilities were also crude and worn out.

Each morning at 7:00 a.m., we would be called to muster outside the barracks for a head count and to receive our instructions for the day. We would hear the "Navy Quote of the Day" and the name of the officer of the day would be announced, after which we would be dismissed. The officers in charge had so few of us to look after that we were left to do as we pleased after morning quarters. Those who continued to stand around would be assigned jobs.

One job assignment that most of us got at least once was walking around the base with a large mattress-size sack and a stick with a nail on the end spearing paper and other trash and placing it in the sack. After a few hours, a gray Chevy pickup truck would come around, and the person picking up the trash would deposit his collection in the open truck bed. The truck would then speed off, redistributing the paper on the side of the road to be picked up again.

I was often able to escape work details by riding the old gray school bus that ran around the base. The bus would stop at two dozen or more stops along the route, even if no one was in sight. Ricky West, whom I had met in electricians' school in Rhode Island, usually rode the bus with me. The rides became so boring that I ventured off base and got a job washing pots and pans and helping cook at the Gulfport Memorial Hospital. One of the men in our group became a postman, and many others had jobs off base. I worked in the hospital for a few months until the number of men sent to Gulfport was sufficient to form a battalion.

Cold or Hot

Ricky West and I had not known that we had both been assigned to MCB 128 until we happened to meet on the base at Gulfport. We arrived in November 1966 and were waiting around until MCB 128 would be reactivated in April. The two of us quickly bonded with our efforts to avoid work details.

As we were riding the bus together, Ricky kept talking about getting married as soon as he had a chance to go back to New Jersey. We were both in somewhat of a panic, realizing the boiling over of the war in Vietnam would soon suck us in.

After a month or so, Ricky managed to get a long weekend. He drove to New Jersey and came back with a bride. While Ricky was gone to get married, I was able to fix up his small house not far from the base. I "acquired" three plates, cups and saucers and silverware from the hospital where I was working. I spoke with some of the civilian ladies on base, who were gracious enough to give me some old drapes for their windows. I also went shopping and bought some groceries, just the essentials to stock the cabinets.

When Ricky and his bride arrived back in Gulfport, they were delighted with their house, but Ricky was obsessed with the notion that now that he was married he did not need to go to war.

As we were both pondering a way not to go to Vietnam, we happened to remember that while we were in school in Rhode Island, there was a chief petty officer who was deploying to the South Pole. The battalion to which the chief petty officer was assigned had construction duties for housing, roads, electrical systems and other infrastructure. The chief had said that there was one billet left for a construction electrician.

Both of us talked about the possibility of escaping Vietnam by going to the South Pole, but since there were two of us and one billet, one of us would have to stay in Gulfport. I decided since Ricky was married and I was not, I should take one for the team and let him go to the Pole.

He filled out the appropriate paper work within a week and requested reassignment to the unit in Rhode Island. Within a few months he was headed back up North to Rhode Island, and my future was sealed.

I never saw Ricky again nor did I ever hear from him. I am sure he must have made at least two deployments to the South Pole.

Work Crew Hideout

Once enough men were on hand at the Gulfport base, we were all given regular job assignments. One of those assignments was to reclaim some of the jungle-like undergrowth of shrubs that covered the outer edges of the back of the base. A large work crew was assembled and dropped off to begin work.

One of our crew was a good old county boy who knew the ropes. He found a large oak tree that had a massive briar patch surrounding it. He cut the briars with his pocket knife, making a tunnel through which we could crawl into a clearing immediately under the tree. This area was very clean with a nice bedding material of old leaves. The whole crew was able to sneak into this space where we took naps, played cards, and quietly spent most of the day relaxing.

The man in charge could be heard walking through the woods calling us, but he could never find us. We were able to keep our little hideout a secret for three days until the amount of work completed did not match the amount of time spent in the woods.

That particular project was short lived as we soon started training. We all suspected that Vietnam was in our future, so my brilliant idea to join the Navy seemed to backfire on me.

Administration Building for Gulfport Seabee Base

Barracks at Gulfport

The Concrete Palace

One of the most interesting beer establishments in Gulfport, Mississippi, in 1966 was a very small, cinder block building on Highway 49, just at the main railroad crossing in town. The only window in the building was the one in front that sported a neon JAX beer sign. Although this was one of the smallest bars in town, it had a certain charm and occasionally offered excitement.

The inside of the building was as plain as the exterior, with one long bar on the right side of the room and two pinball machines to the left. The pinball machines would pay money to those who were patient enough to play. I never was.

The building had a dirt floor which was decorated with various brands of cigarette filters. There were several small round tables around the room and one door in the rear that had a restroom sign on it. The door opened to the outside. One had to be careful as the railroad tracks were just a few feet from that door.

On a few occasions, there would be entertainment in the palace when two "career" women came in about the same time and got into a fight over their chosen "date." The ensuing wrestling match was a forerunner of today's mud wrestling. The girls would be covered in the floor dirt and

would usually be perspiring. All in all, it was very entertaining and nothing like anything I had ever experienced
back home.

Sadly, Hurricane Camille came four years later and took
that grand palace away. Now, only the memories remain.

Dining Hall on Base at Gulfport

The Gulfport Crew

The military is an amazing place to see society in all its glory. The cast of characters in Gulfport was all inclusive from the good, the bad, and the ugly.

One character I remember is Albert Neeves from North Carolina. Albert had no front teeth and was as hard as a rock. He was a mountain man who enjoyed women, whiskey, and fighting.

One day Albert wanted to borrow a motorcycle from one of the guys who had just purchased a 650cc Honda Scrambler. The owner, a very likable, free-hearted fellow, gave Albert the keys. Albert roared off on Friday around noon and was not seen again until Monday morning about 6:00 a.m.

When Albert finally pulled up to the barracks, there were two glass gallon jugs tied to the back of the motorcycle. Albert had gone to North Carolina for the weekend and brought two gallons of moonshine back with him. He also told about paying a visit to his best friend's wife since his friend had been out of town, and the wife was lonely.

On the afternoon of his arrival back at the base, Albert bought a case of pint mason jars and filled them with his shine. When I asked him what he was doing, he said he

21

was going to hide the jars around the base just in case he was on a work detail and needed a drink.

There were four or five Native Americans from the Great Plains in our battalion. One of them named St. Germain was a beautiful example of the way an Indian should look. However, St. Germain was on a self-destructive course, reckless with women and always drunk.

Leonard Farabee, from Alexandria, Louisiana, was another interesting person with whom I shared a barracks in Gulfport. Leonard was about five-feet, six- inches tall and weighed about two hundred ten pounds. He smoked Raleigh cigarettes because on the back of each pack there was a coupon that was redeemable for free gifts. I often told Leonard that he could get an iron lung with his coupons.

Since Leonard was very quiet, I decided he was a good companion with whom I could go to town. On one of our excursions, we went to a local beer joint and drank Vodka Collins and other exotic drinks. Even though I was only nineteen, it didn't seem to matter to the people at the bar. No one ever asked me to prove that I was old enough to purchase alcohol.

As Leonard and I were enjoying our drinks, much to our surprise, two women walked out on a makeshift stage and began dancing. I never knew the human pelvis could do such things. I don't think I even took a drink during the entertainment. I must have looked like a country boy with my mouth open and eyes bugged out of my head. This was the first of many of my worldly educational experiences in the Navy.

When there were enough warm bodies to form a battalion, we were commissioned MCB 128 on April 1, 1967. Our training would soon start in earnest for our ultimate destination, Vietnam.

With more men on base, the opportunities to learn about life increased. Life was full of adventures both on and off base, with every day bringing new surprises.

Lou in Gulfport

Albert Neeves on Motorcycle in Vietnam

The Cotton Club

Conversations in the barracks were always a stimulus to get involved and learn about things that were not common to my upbringing. One of those conversations occurred shortly after my arrival at the newly reopened base in Gulfport. The topic of the discussion was an off-the-beaten-path establishment north of Gulfport called The Cotton Club.

The club was located off the main road on an oyster shell road that was nearly a mile long. As the road wound westward, the area became wilder with marshes, low shrubs, and small trees.

The building spoke of grand days gone by when it was once a classy spot in the country where the elite could dine in comfort. Some twenty years back, The Cotton Club had been an upscale dining and dancing facility, but it was now reduced to a dirty bar with an adjoining closed restaurant.

The exterior of the building needed painting, and worn out boards needed to be replaced. The club was designated as "off limits" because of the filth and isolation and the possibility of altercations with local patrons.

The first area upon entering was a bar crowded with beer drinkers. The place needed a good cleaning, but that seemed low on the owner's "to do" list. There was an archway to the left that led into the once plush dining area filled with dirty, red booths where some of the previous night's patrons were sleeping off a good drunk. But that didn't seem to be bothering anyone.

On the particular night I decided to check out The Cotton Club, the place was filled with many familiar faces from the base. I was about to start my second beer when the Shore Patrol came bursting in the front door to round us up. The Shore Patrol was our military "super cops" whose job it was to enforce the off limits regulations. There was a human explosion of half-drunk patrons trying to escape the grasp of the "law." I ran out the back door and dove into a six-foot-tall pile of cans and bottles which had been left by years of reveling. The Shore Patrol officers came out the door, looked around, and promptly went back inside to round up less agile offenders.

As I lay in the huge pile of cans, small amounts of stale beer that had percolated in the hot southern sun began to run down my back, and I became drenched. I walked several miles to the base because cab drivers would not transport me after they got a whiff. Once back on the base, I discarded my rancid smelling clothes and checked The Cotton Club off my list of places to visit in Gulfport. I never ventured there again.

Night with a Cat

One October day, while I was training in Gulfport, I was in the barracks fooling around with a fake British accent when Tom Utterback from Indiana heard me. He came over and asked me to help him play a trick on his girlfriend. I, being easily corruptible, agreed.

Tom had a huge, white Lincoln Continental and played the "big shot" role nicely. He decided to tell his girlfriend that I was a British officer, whom the commanding officer of our base wanted him to entertain while in the States.

We arrived at his girlfriend's house, where Tom introduced me as Officer Timkins. All went well until the lady's two young boys came home from playing and started to marvel at this strange talking man.

The boys quickly dug through their record pile and found a recording of "The Battle of New Orleans" where Colonel Jackson defeated the British army. I had to pretend to be offended and put up quite an argument. The young boys delighted in needling me, and we all had fun.

Finally, we left the house so that I could be driven around and shown the many "sights" of the area.

Louis Remmers

While we were stopped at a red light near Biloxi, I noticed that the young woman sitting in the car next to ours was dressed in a cat suit, complete with whiskers, ears, and a tight fitting black costume.

The woman rolled down her car window and asked if we knew where there was a Halloween party in the area. Tom offered her my company in her quest for a party, so I, Officer Timkins, went with the cat woman. After she drove around for about two hours and didn't find a party, the kitty invited me to go home with her. I accepted the invitation, not realizing she was from Mobile, Alabama.

When we arrived at her house, I was introduced to the couch in the living room where I woke up about 6:00 the next morning. The young lady, now in regular attire, came down from her bedroom and made me a cup of awful tasting instant coffee. She informed me that she had things to do and that I needed to leave.

I had duty in Gulfport that night, so I walked, jogged, ran, and hitchhiked back to the base. My duty time began at 6:00 p.m., and I arrived exhausted in the barracks about 5:15 p.m.

I no longer wanted to be a British officer. The work was just too taxing.

Diving School

In late December 1966, our battalion in Gulfport, MCB 128, was close to a full complement and getting ready to be deployed to Vietnam. One morning as we mustered up near the chow hall, the officer of the day asked if anyone wanted to volunteer to become a diver for the battalion. I decided that might be a fun experience, so I volunteered.

There were three diving schools to which we might be sent for training, and one was near Washington DC, which was within easy traveling distance to my family. If I could get an assignment there, I would have a chance to spend some weekends at home. The second school was in San Diego, California, and the third in the Philippines.

Before any training or assignments, all the volunteers were given aptitude tests, and some of the guys were culled during this process. Next came the swimming test, which was held in an outdoor private pool in Ocean Springs, Mississippi, in the middle of January. Because of the bitter cold and the filthy water, we lost many more of the volunteers that day.

The number dropped from the original fifty-five applicants to six of us who made the grade to be trained Navy divers. As luck would have it, I didn't get to go anyplace near home as I had hoped. I received my orders to report to diving school in San Diego the following June.

When my group of diving trainees arrived in San Diego, we were assigned to an off-base barracks that was on top of a hill overlooking the harbor. On the first day we reported with twenty in our class and were quickly informed that we now belonged to the diving instructors. We were issued diving manuals and listened to a lecture. Then we went outside to the diving barge.

We were lined up on the seawall and told to swim out to a buoy in the harbor. From where we were standing, the buoy looked deceivingly small, but it was actually at least twenty feet across.

The instructors stood and watched as we swam two by two to the buoy and back. Our arrival back at the sea wall determined how we would be matched with one another to form two-man teams. I placed second out of twenty swimmers.

After we had completed the swim, we lined up side-by-side with our partners and ran five miles to an area south of the base where tailings of harbor dredging were piled. These were hills at least five stories high of very soft sandy material on which we exercised. That day we lost two of our group because they threw up or passed out.

Every day, we lined up and ran. The running was followed by calisthenics, after which we ran to the diving barge. Upon reaching the barge, we went to classes on diving physics, diving techniques, or some other pertinent diving information, before we hit the water.

The Pacific Ocean in San Diego was very cold and could

sap one's energy very quickly. Once we got into condition, we started diving activities. All of our training activities were timed. If our assigned tasks were not completed with the given time limit, we had to hit the deck to do twenty pushups and twenty sit-ups. The more we trained, the shorter the amount of time we were given to complete our tasks.

Most of the training involved the use of a hard hat suit which weighed two hundred ten pounds dry. The gear was made of copper, and the helmet weighed fifty-four pounds. A weight belt was eighty-five pounds and each shoe was twenty pounds. The hoses and the connection gear made up the remaining weight. As we dressed in this outfit, each two-man team would be timed. If either member of the team exceeded the time limit, both team members had to hit the deck for pushups.

After we dressed in our suits and our helmets were screwed in place with the front windows open, one of the diving instructors would smoke a cigar and blow smoke into our faces just before closing the windows. There was no air flow into the suit until we reached the water so our only means of getting air until the dive began was a small one-eighth inch cock on the side of the helmet. The windows in our helmets would fog up, and we were completely out of breath before reaching the water when we were able to open a valve and get a breath of fresh air. This was done to limit the amount of oxygen and to stress the divers to see if we would panic.

One training activity involved building a "bird house" under water, using six square pieces of wood of equal

size, nails and a rope used to hold the bundle of wood together. The trick was to nail the boards together without
allowing them to float to the surface. This had to be done
while wearing a hard hat.

Another training activity was to go down a descending
line about a hundred yards long that ran on an angle off
the back of the dive barge. We were to go hand-over-hand
down the line adjusting the air flow in our suits until we
reached the bottom.

One of the class members could not adjust his air flow
properly and lost his grip causing him to fall to the bottom. This ruptured both of his eardrums, and yet another
member left our class.

About two weeks into the training, we began running the
five miles carrying a telephone pole over our heads. Pain
was the norm as we strained with all our might just to
keep up. To help distract us from the agony, we chanted
and sang as we ran, but our lungs burned anyway.

The intense training pushed us to our limits. On several
occasions, the instructor ran us to a garbage dumpster and
had us crawl through from one side to the other. The ones
who came out not covered with maggots had to crawl
through again before the run would resume.

One day, twenty army trainees showed up to learn scuba
diving. Our instructor had had a wisdom tooth extracted
the previous day and did not feel well, so my partner, Kathen Caddy, and I offered to run the first day of training
with the new arrivals. All twenty army recruits quit and

failed to show up for their second day. After our day as trainers, Caddy, and I had several days of pushups and sit-ups to make amends for agitating the troops.

Caddy and I worked hard to become one. The more the instructors rode us, the harder we resisted. When he would mess up and had to do pushups, I joined him and vice versa. We were soon challenging our instructors by asking if we could do fifteen pushups while standing on our hands rather than doing twenty regular. The instructors thought we were crazy, but we were getting stronger and shrugging off all the torture.

"Hell Week" began about halfway through our training and was designed to shake out the less than dedicated students. It was a ratchet up from all the physical and mental challenges we had already endured. Some days, we were in the ocean until we could not stop shaking from the bone cold. On other days, we were in the Olympic-size pool on the base where we swam around the perimeter of the pool in scuba gear. The instructors would attack us and dislodge our breathing apparatus, trying to disorient us. We were forced to keep our composure enough to get the gear back on and operating properly.

One day as we were swimming around the bottom of the pool in full gear, the base commander's daughter thought she would go for a swim. The pool was closed for our sessions, but she was under the impression that she was special. The young lady wasn't very attractive and had a major attitude problem. All the men in the pool watched as she began swimming around using a frog kick.

Caddy and I had the same idea at the same time—to give the commander's daughter an attitude adjustment. We both swam under her and allowed our scuba gear to free flow air which released a large belch of air under her pelvis. There was a scream, and she abruptly left the pool. We heard that there was some irritation from the men in charge, but there was also a prevailing atmosphere of "Atta Boy."

We were told that we could break for some games. We were given standard issue towels and made to race from one end of the pool to the other with each swimmer holding the end of a towel. Pulling wet towels through the water was very painful on our arms. Winners made laps around the pool while losers hit the deck for pushups and sit-ups.

After that activity, we would play a game called "In the Pool, Out of the Pool." When an instructor would blow a whistle we would jump into the pool and then climb out as quickly as possible. This would go on until someone could no longer pull himself out. Then we were all punished by doing pushups and sit-ups.

We trained from 6:00 a.m. until 7:00 p.m. with a twenty minute break for lunch and bathroom breaks. When I arrived at the barracks, I sometimes sat down on my empty bunk and woke up the next morning stiff and sore all over but ready to go again.

On the next to the last day of "Hell Week," one of our members from MCB 128, Ozzie Baldaris, announced, "I may drink, smoke, and take dope, but I am no fool. I quit this stuff." Remarkable thinking!

Three officers came by and pulled Caddy and me out of class. They interviewed us then separated us to have further discussions.

After chow that evening, Caddy and I discussed our interviews. The officers were trying to recruit us for a new group called "Seals." We had both refused with identical excuses. We intended to return to Gulfport and rejoin MCB 128. The officers came back on two other occasions to convince us to join, but we declined to volunteer.

By the time our training had finished, our class of twenty had dwindled down to four. I was second in my class behind my partner, Kathen Caddy.

We had set records for all the required tasks and were interviewed on three separate occasions to see what made us tick. We were just two energetic kids pushing back whatever was being pushed our way.

The diving experience made us mentally and physically tough, and we were able to do whatever we were called on to do without very much difficulty. As grueling as the training was, it was made easier by our determination to show that we could prevail.

Lou at Diving School

Jack Brown Rig for Shallow Diving

My Diving Partner, Kathen Caddy

Descending Line on an Angle

Training to be a Diver

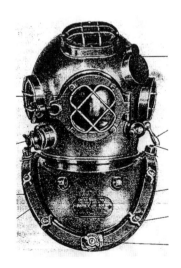

Diving Helmet

Shave Like a Man

Kathen Caddy and I had been in diving school for nearly three weeks and were enjoying the nightlife around San Diego. Our barracks were located about a quarter of a mile north of the main base where we were stationed.

One Monday morning after a full weekend of fun, we were running late and arrived at the main gate to find a brand new PFC Marine on guard. The Marine told us that we were not in uniform since we were not clean shaven, so we would not be able to enter the base. Since both Caddy and I had very blonde hair, we did not shave very often.

Time was running short, and we did not have enough time to go back to the barracks, shave, and then come back for breakfast if we were to make it to the diving barge on time. There was a drug store about halfway between the barracks and the base, so we ran to the store and pooled our loose change to buy a razor. However, we did not have enough money for shaving cream.

Caddy and I ran back to the gate and stood in front of the guard shack and started dry shaving. We tore the flesh on our chins until we were bleeding, but we were not going to let that Marine guard get the best of us.

Caddy would shave some of his face and then give me the razor. I would shave some on my face and give the razor back to Caddy. We passed the razor back and forth until we were finished. The Marine watched in shock but let us pass without a word.

As we were diving later that day, the salt water from the ocean reminded us of our foolishness.

Caddy and Lou

Eat Like You Can

The chow hall on the naval base in San Diego was on the second floor of a large building. There were ramps that went from the ground level to the main entrance. The chow line usually moved rapidly up the ramps, and we would get our food and be seated in a reasonable amount of time.

One afternoon as Caddy and I were standing on the ramp and waiting in the line for lunch, some snappy Marines appeared escorting a line of young soldiers from the brig, a jailhouse for sailors. As this group approached, all of the people who were waiting in line behind Caddy and me moved to the side to allow the prisoners to pass and take their place at the front.

When Caddy saw what was happening, he decided to make a statement by leaning across the walkway and stretching his arms over to the wall. I took the adjacent wall so that we had the ramp fully blocked.

When the prisoners got to where we were standing, they stopped. Caddy announced that we had been working all morning and had not been in jail so we were going to eat before the losers from jail.

Not a word was spoken, and we ate before the prisoners and Marines that day.

Louis Remmers

Divers' Training

42

Party Poopers

While in San Diego for diving school, Caddy and I and a fellow Seabee named Habecker usually ate together. One night as Caddy, Habecker, and I were leaving the chow hall after finishing our evening meal, we ran into a Marine from Habecker's hometown. The Marine was surprised to see his high school classmate in San Diego and invited him to a party that night. We were also invited, and as any twenty-year-olds would, we decided to go. We were to meet at the front gate of the base and take a cab to the party.

We met the cab at the appointed time and ended up in the enlisted men's family complex, a series of several three story brick buildings all exactly alike in neat rows. We were dropped off in front of one of the three story buildings, and all four of us went up to the second floor.

Habecker's Marine friend knocked, and the door opened to a less than neat and clean apartment. The grossly overweight woman who opened the door was wearing an old dress and smoking a cigarette. On her hip was a young baby, who was coughing and sneezing, an obvious indication of an allergic reaction from the smoke. The child had sores on his legs from insect bites and was crying.

The woman invited us in and called three other young ladies from the back of the apartment to come see us. The lady who had opened the door left to take the baby downstairs to be cared for while she partied.

We were all introduced to the young ladies from the back room and were underwhelmed. My "date" was wearing a light blue dress that needed washing. The hem of the dress had come out, making it a little rough around the edges.

The girl was anxious to party and started small talk while leading me to a room. As I looked back I noticed all the ladies were escorting their dates to bedrooms.

I was instructed to lie down on a single bed, and my date lay beside me, continuing with the small talk. I knew what was up and was not interested, so I said that I was hungry. Without hesitation, the girl reached under the bed and retrieved a large bowl of potato chips that from the appearance of the bowl had been there for some time.

After a few minutes, I told the girl I needed to go to the bathroom and would be right back. I made a beeline for the front door and bumped into Caddy, who was also making a quick exit. We were so connected that we again both had the same idea at the same time ... GET OUT OF TOWN! Those women were wives of sailors who were deployed on ships in the Pacific Ocean.

We laughed all the way back to the base, but Habecker was not very pleased with us for upsetting the evening's party atmosphere. Habecker soon dropped out of diving school, and we never connected again.

Too Many Shots

I returned from diving school in San Diego and reunited with B Company of MCB 128 in Gulfport. The battalion had been training for our deployment to Vietnam, and I was a little behind in the training. After a week of catching up with my buddies, one morning I got a call from sick bay ordering me to report to the base hospital for some reason unknown to me.

When I arrived at the base hospital, I was informed that I had not been getting my required immunizations for deployment to Southeast Asia, and I had to catch up on those also. This didn't concern me very much until I realized I had been away for more than twelve weeks, and the hospital corpsman informed me that the rest of the men from MCB 128 had gotten at least two shots a week for the entire time I had been gone.

I was escorted into a small room where there were three corpsmen. I removed my shirt, and they proceeded to give me injections, one after another in both arms. This continued for what seemed to be an eternity. I began to get a little weak in the knees since it was taking so long to complete the job. I received shots for typhus, typhoid, cholera, plague, and the list went on until all the shots that I had missed had been administered.

I got dressed and returned to the barracks but did not feel too well. I soon had a fever and chills along with severe aching.

My arms began to swell so much that I had to remove my shirt. In a short time, I could hardly move my arms above my waist, and I could not sit down. I walked up and down the main aisle of the barracks for nearly ten hours. My buddies in the barracks advised me to go to the sick bay for help, but that is where I got in trouble in the first place. For several days, I was incredibly sore all over. If I had not just returned from the rigorous training of diving school, I might not have survived the onslaught to my immune system. The guys working in sick bay had only been concerned with getting their paper work up to speed with no thought as to the consequences of so many immunizations.

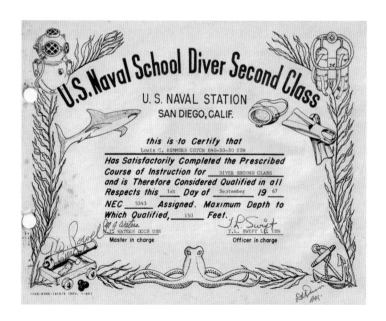

Training at Camp LeJeune

In September 1967, my Seabee battalion, MCB 128, was sent to Camp LeJeune for Marine infantry training prior to our deployment to Vietnam. As we deplaned from our C130 cargo plane and stepped onto North Carolina soil, the Marines watched with dismay and disgust. We were dressed in Marine greens, yet our clothing was the only thing about our appearance that spoke of anything military.

Our training at Camp LeJeune rotated from one area to the next. One day we were sent to the machine gun range. We were all familiar with the M60 machine gun as we had been through the rifle range training at Keesler Air Force Base near Biloxi, Mississippi, several months earlier. We were all given a chance to fire the machine gun from the prone position.

The firing range was on a small rise and the targets were nearly one hundred yards down range. The company of men was stationed behind the rise in the land, and each soldier was summoned when it was his turn to fire the gun.

One of my friends who had been steadily getting more anxious about our mission was Leonard Farabee from Louisiana and whom I had met in Gulfport. Leonard had been losing weight at an alarming rate and had been less talkative as he contemplated our fate.

When Leonard was called up, he assumed the prone position, pulled the trigger and panicked. The rapid firing of the machine gun caused Leonard to stand up, and the gun recoil caused it to climb into the air. Soon we were all running for cover and hiding behind pine trees. A marine sergeant tackled Leonard and twisted the belt of bullets, jamming the gun and causing it to stop firing. Everyone in the company was quite shook up, and Leonard was escorted by two Marines to the sick bay where he was treated for a case of the nerves.

The very next day, B Company was sent to the hand grenade range for more training. The contour of the land was the same with pine trees behind the range and a gentle rise in the land with horseshoe shaped bunkers big enough for three men to stand in. When grenades were thrown, the participants were to duck behind the bunkers before the grenade could go off. One by one we took turns, and the boring day seemed to drag on until Leonard had his turn. As expected, Leonard dropped the grenade, and the instructor had to recover the mistake before disaster struck.

The men in the company became restless during the hot wait, and all sorts of games were started. Some men threw knives at targets, and some threw them at others' feet and at each other. Other men played games of catch-me-if-you-can, and some wrestled over left over cake one fellow had stuffed into his pockets. As we entertained ourselves, the grenades would boom and small fragments of steel would trickle through the trees and onto our heads.

A new supply of grenades was delivered in a five-ton truck, and the wooden boxes in which they were packed fell apart when they were being unloaded. On close examination, we noticed that the munitions had World War II dates on the boxes.

As the day wore on, we realized that nearly every fourth grenade failed to go off. We were instructed to keep our heads down while a young Marine went out in the field to retrieve the failed grenade and gently roll it into a hole designated for disposal. The courage of the young Marine amazed us.

The following day, we were in full gear for what was to be a four-day walk in the woods. We walked to a designated area, set up camp, waited for the Marines to attack us. We dug in as instructed. In true Seabee fashion, some of the fortifications were amazing. One group of men made recliners out of dirt in their fighting holes, while other made elaborate shelters with pine branch roofs. Some dug connection trenches so card games could be played at night without being discovered by the brass.

Most men complained about their feet hurting from the march. But as usual, our complaints were dismissed by the officers. One by one, the men removed their boots to find them filled with blood. The new issue boots had the heels put on with nails that were so long they had come though the soles and into the foot-bed of the boots. The whole battalion was out of commission.

The Marines came in a convoy of trucks to get us and take us back to civilization and comfortable barracks. We were all given slippers which further confused the hard-nosed Marines all around us.

It took two days of rest for most of the wounds on our feet to heal enough for us to continue with our training, but we enjoyed the free time. New boots were issued, and we never were marched into the woods again. Some speculated it was the Marines decision while others thought it was our officers who finally saw the futility in what we were doing.

Rifle Launched Grenades

Pop Up Target Practice

After we settled in at Camp LeJeune, our battalion was split up and sent to various educational settings to make us into men like our brother Marines. Company B, of which I was a member, was divided in half. Sixty men were sent to class while I and fifty-nine others were sent to the combat pop up target range.

Each one in my assigned group arrived at the target range with an AR15 rifle and three empty ammunition clips that would hold twenty shots apiece. We were briefed by a Marine sergeant and given the sixty bullets needed to fill our clips. Five men at a time would be ushered to the starting area where they were to go on patrol. As the patrol wound its way through the woods, targets would randomly appear, first on one side and then the other. When this happened, we were to dive to the ground and fire at the targets. When a target was hit enough times, it would fall down, and we would proceed along the trail until the next target appeared. The patrols took turns until it was apparent that everyone knew when and where the targets would appear. Then boredom set in.

One member of our company decided to bring a little excitement to the group by sharing his clips with his buddies. This idea caught on, and all of a sudden each member of the patrol had at least nine clips for a total of one hundred eighty bullets. As a target popped up, it was riddled with automatic fire and very soon was in shreds. By the time the Marine in charge realized what was happening, the targets were completely ruined. We were all commanded to stand at attention until our security officer was summoned.

In short order, a jeep driven by a Marine corporal came roaring through the woods. In it was riding Lieutenant Chiomento, our security officer. The Lieutenant had no trouble reprimanding us by the book as he was a "Frank Burns" type, made famous in later years by the TV program M.A.S.H.

Next, the Marine who had been in charge of our pop-up training took his turn chewing us out in very unsavory language. He then requested a private chat with Lieutenant Chiomento. It happened that I had a spare purple smoke bomb in my possession, so while they were talking, I slipped out of the ranks and wired the bomb to the jeep's frame and attached a long trip wire made of steel to the drive shaft of the jeep. I slipped back into the ranks just as the conference was finished and in time for dismissal.

Lieutenant Chiomento climbed into the jeep and was driven off into the woods. We all counted to ten after which we heard the distinctive "POP" of the grenade and watched the woods fill with purple smoke.

Lieutenant Chiomento, shoulders set and fists clinched, stomped back to our position, and we were again quickly mustered up at attention. Lieutenant Chiomento questioned all of us for nearly an hour before he gave up and left the area.

No one ever told on my misconduct. We all enjoyed the prank, and our security officer had a lovely purple jeep.

Nearly at Attention at Camp LeJeune, USMC

Antique WWII Bazooka

Rifle Range

Off to War

Our training had finally been completed, and we were waiting to be shipped out to the war in Vietnam. As the reality of what was about to happen sank in, an uneasy silence seemed to take over the men of MCB 128. All the fun and games were over, and the time had come to face the fact that we were off to war.

We and our AR-15 rifles with no ammunition were loaded on large five-ton trucks for our trip to the airport. As we exited the truck and lined up to board the plane, the sun striking the big silver bird made it impossible to see where we were walking. Our sea bags, which were big, green, heavy sacks filled with all our worldly possessions, were placed on large pallets and put on the back of the huge C-141 airplane.

The plane had rows of seats facing the rear. The inside was dark, with the only source of light being a few ceiling fixtures. Did the military mess up or were civilian flyers able to demand better accommodations? The doors closed. The engines whined, and we were on our way.

Boredom soon set in, and it's never a good idea to bore Seabees. There were four doors with small portholes in each door of this aircraft, and we were soon taking turns warming them with the palms of our hands in order to melt the frost and get a glimpse of the land below. If the line got too long, the plane would gently tilt, and the pilot would make a correction. Soon, we all began messing with the pilot by moving to various areas of the cabin, causing the plane to fly erratically. After a while, a member of the flight crew came to the back and told us that we all had to sit down.

Our first stop was Alaska, where we touched down on a frozen runway. We had left Gulfport, Mississippi, where the weather is warm and sunny in October, and now we were amazed to be in a place where the snow could be measured in feet.

While we were in Alaska, one of the cooks in our outfit had his family meet us at the air base. We were all excited about meeting his family and thought it was a great treat to have them there to see us off. Most of us didn't even know that he was from Alaska.

Our aircraft was refueled, and we were fed. After a few hours, we were again on our way.

Thirty hours passed from the time we left our home base in Gulfport until our plane was on its final decent to Da Nang Air Base in South Vietnam. The glide path of the plane was unusual. The closer we got to touch down, the more the nose dipped down. We were told that the purpose of this was to prevent being hit by ground fire from small arms in the jungle.

The plane's two right engines were shut down as we taxied to an open area. The front door was opened, and we were hurried out the door which was on the right side, while a forklift quickly unloaded our bags from the rear.

When the plane was emptied, it turned and flew away leaving us to fight a war.

The heat and stench were overwhelming. The air and our nerves made us all queasy. Our spirits sank.

We were ushered to a large area between two buildings where several trucks and trailers were waiting for us. The trailers, normally used by movers, had windows too high for us to stand and look out at the land, but we could look up and see the night sky.

As the truck rolled down the roads, we looked up through those windows to watch flares, planes, and helicopters flying in all directions. We were troubled about seeing that much activity at 3:00a.m. but would soon come to understand that it was the norm and not an exception.

When we finally arrived at Camp Faulkner, our new home, we were covered with sweat and dirt. We were assigned hooches and were amazed that we never saw any of the men we were replacing. The hooches were clean and empty and not a soul was around. This made the situation even more unnerving to most of us.

Sleep did not come that first night as we were all gazing at the flares and planes in the sky. Rumbling of bombs and occasional rifle shots could be heard throughout the night. We were scared. None of us ever imagined anything like this.

Loading Up to Leave for Vietnam

Saying Goodbye

Earning a Gold Ribbon

The long training and preparation for our deployment in Vietnam made an unusual fraternity of all of the men of MCB 128. We had been through a lot together and shared good times and bad times and now were deployed.

The anxiety was at an all-time high when we noticed that the marines with whom we were associated all seemed to have a small ribbon in the air vents of their hats. The ribbon was slender gold with black lines for borders. We were intrigued with this apparent departure from the squared away military bearing of the marines.

One day I asked a marine about the neat bow tied in his hat, and he informed me that it was a silent protest against the war. When I asked where the ribbons came from, I was informed they came from the neck of a bottle of Canadian Mist Whiskey.

The marine told me that if you could drink the bottle of whiskey within twenty-four hours, you could remove the ribbon from the bottle and tie a neat bow in the hat you were issued, and unless you were being inspected, no one seemed to care.

I decided that I needed to be a part of this grand rebellion, so I used my ration cards to get a bottle of whiskey. Sure enough, I saw the ribbon wrapped around the neck of the bottle and held in place under the label. One night I began drinking, and the whiskey tasted terrible. I had never tasted whiskey, but the peer pressure was too great to stop. I forced down every swallow of the nasty stuff, and late the next day, drunk as a skunk, I was able to retrieve my ribbon.

The following day at morning quarters, we were given malaria wafers and told to take them right away to prevent malaria. I took mine and within a few hours I was very ill.

Company B of MCB 128 was made up of plumbers and electricians so we were the only company area in camp to have real toilets and showers. The toilets were lined up in the traditional military row that made it very handy for my illness. I spent all night between toilets, leaning over one toilet as the whiskey purged my upper GI system and then leaning back and clearing my lower GI system from the diarrhea caused by the malaria tablets.

It took me three days to rehydrate. I never remember being issued malaria tablets again, probably because all of company B had a negative reaction to the medications.

The Electric Chair

For my first job, I was assigned to the command post, the electrical and communications center of MCB 128, our Seabee battalion while in Vietnam. My responsibility was keeping the telephones and the PRC-25 radios working. There was always someone assigned to that job so we worked day and night on rotating shifts.

The command post facility was underground beneath the battalion's clerical offices. It consisted of two rooms, an outer room with a half door leading into the inner room that housed the radio and telephone equipment. The two rooms were about eight feet wide and nearly twenty feet long and were finished in early American plywood. At the end of the second room, there was a large window air conditioner which was necessary to keep the oppressive humidity from ruining the radios. The average daytime temperature in the bunker was about eighty-five degrees Fahrenheit, but the humidity was low compared to the ninety percent outside. The air in the bunker had been re-circulated for so long that it smelled like it had been there for a decade.

In spite of the stale air, we often had visits from officers who would come in to pass time and soak up the cooler, drier air. Many of them puffed on cheap cigars leaving an odor that lingered for days. Some of my fellow workers and I came up with a plan to correct that problem.

We scrounged around at the air base and found a nice chrome chair which we placed at the end of the room under the air conditioner. I ran a wire from the chair, inside the wall, upstairs to the offices. Then, I installed a switch at a desk upstairs that connected the wire to ninety volts of DC current, normal ringing current. When an officer would come in and sit down in the chair, I would call up to the office which housed the switch, and a helpful clerk would count to ten and turn on the current. The unsuspecting officer would receive a hard jolt of electricity which usually made him momentarily stand at attention.

The officer would then inquire about the cause of his shock so we made up a story about humidity, skin resistance, and induced electrical fields from the electronic equipment. Our explanation, that a "capacitor reaction" would electrify the human body for several days thereby causing electrical shocks by touching anything metal including toothpaste, resulted in the a rapid departure from the bunker and seemed to satisfy the unknowing.

The visits by officers to the bunker soon began to taper off until we were left alone to perform our duty in what we called "peace" and without cigars.

A Break in the Darkness

In December 1967, while I was working the switch board in the command post, two Seabees came for a visit. I recognized them as divers who were in the class behind me in diving school. They had come to tell me that Roger Huestis[1] had been killed in a mortar attack.

It was amazing that these two had been able to locate me and were thoughtful enough to come to give me the news. However, I wished they had not. I was speechless from shock. For days, my depression worsened. I was unable to believe that one of my friends was gone.

I had last seen Roger in August. He had been the number three diver in my class of only four graduates. Now after all we had gone through, Roger was dead.

Roger was only twenty years old and had been in Nam for three months. I kept remembering all the things we endured together and realized he was a tougher person than I. He just didn't have a diving partner like Caddy. Having Caddy around gave me strength to carry on.

_____

[1] Roger Edward Huestis, North Merrick, NY, 01/27/1947-
12/14/1967, Wall Panel 31E, Line 092

A week or two after Roger's passing, I was doing repair work outside when I heard someone say that Bob Hope was putting on a USO show at the DaNang Air Base. I made a beeline to the show and, with tool pouch and flak jacket, blended in with thousands of soldiers.

When Bob Hope finally came on stage, we all erupted in applause and cheering. All during the show I kept thinking about how I had never realized what a short person Hope was. From my distant vantage point, he appeared to be about six inches tall.

The show was lots of music, dance, and, of course, several beautiful girls. It felt like magic just to be there and think that these celebrities could give so much of their time for us. For a few minutes it was almost possible to forget the pain and the circumstances that brought me there.

The show was over far too quickly, and at the end, we all sang *Silent Night* which brought tears to the eyes of every young man who was there.

I slowly made my way back east across the river to our camp at Da Nang. I didn't talk too much about the show because I wasn't sure how it would set with those who could not escape for the afternoon. That Christmas event was the single ray of light in an otherwise dark deployment.

Goat or Hero

In January 1968, I was working in the command post, the electrical and communications heart of our battalion. I sat in front of four stacks of telephone switchboards that were the old plug type. To my left was a single side-band radio that was used on a weekly basis to contact any unit in Vietnam that had the correct frequency and call signs. To my right on the wall was a grid map of the area we called "home." Directly behind me was a set of five PRC-25 radios that were backup communications for our perimeter security force.

I worked on rotating shifts which were twelve hours, sixteen hours, and the longest one, eighteen hours. The twelve hour day was six hours in the bunker, three hours off, and then six on again. The sixteen hour day was eight on, three off and then eight on again. The eighteen hour day was six in the bunker, six on repair of phone lines wherever they were down, and six back in the bunker. -

About the first month I was there, the commanding officer, Commander Wittschiebe, sent a memo to the bunker saying the person on duty must call him to ask for permission prior to firing any flares or mortars. Our mortar crew usually fired flares to light up the sky if our security company wanted a better look at the jungle. We had two crews that could hit a gnat a mile away before you could blink an eye.

One night, I was following a Marine patrol's progress on the map board in the bunker. We used a system of clicks on the radio from the patrol to me to indicate various check points along the trail so I knew exactly where they were located at every moment. This backup system was used to get the patrol rapid help when it was needed.

On that particular night, a five-man Marine patrol was out setting up an ambush for the Viet Cong who were reported to be in the area and suspected of getting a rocket attack in place to hit the Da Nang airbase. Our patrol was doing its job, and I had its location in place on the map from the radio clicks that were being transmitted.

Sure enough, the VC came calling. Although the Marines didn't know it at the time, there were a dozen more VC than expected, and the Marines were greatly outnumbered.

The Marine on the radio yelled for help, and I called the mortar crews for fire. I then called the old man to ask for permission. By the time the commander's phone rang, the rounds were already in the air.

The commander soon honored me with a personal visit that lasted for several hours filled with yelling, cursing, and smoke being blown in my face. I was in real trouble. The Marines, however, had been able to fight off the attack because they could see the enemy. They all returned back to their base safely.

Three days later, a full bird colonel from the Marine battalion came into our outer room asking to speak to Commander Wittschiebe. I called the commander, and he came to the bunker to meet the colonel. The Marine colonel asked the commander who was on duty the night his patrol was fired on, and the commander turned to me and pointed and said, "It was he."

The colonel opened a small box which contained a medal he wished to present to me for my fast action in saving his patrol. My commander was furious at this and told the colonel that I would not be getting any medal as I did not follow orders.

The colonel objected and indicated that if the flares had not been fired when they were, his patrol would have been lost. Commander Wittschiebe, told the colonel he could leave because the conversation was finished.

I learned a valuable lesson that day. It was perceived by those in command to be more important to follow orders than to act quickly and save lives.

The Flares Being Fired

Working in the Command Post

Big Stink Job

Since I was also a Navy diver, I was required to work in that capacity every six months. I took leave of the command post and went to work on the diving barge in Da Nang harbor. Caddy also went to dive at the same time so that our Team #1 was back together. The diving was non-stop and averaged from eight to ten hours a day.

Large cargo ships came into the harbor with supplies and ammunition for the war effort. On one occasion, a ship was unloading generators on pallets, and one of the cables snapped causing four generators to fall overboard.

A call came in to the diving barge to send someone to retrieve the generators, so I volunteered to go. When I arrived at the cargo ship, I went onboard to inspect the generators to see what I was going to be diving to find. After seeing the magnitude of the job, I decided it was a hard hat job and sent for a heavy diving rig.

The hard hat diving rigs at the time consisted of a copper helmet that weighed fifty-five pounds, two boots that were twenty pounds each, and an eighty-four pound weighed belt to go around the waist. The diver would suit up in a canvas and rubber outfit followed by the boots and helmet.

When my rig arrived, I suited up and rode a line some forty feet through the murky water and then another twenty-five feet into ancient mud. The visibility was virtually zero as I groped along in filth that was as thick as chocolate pudding. Being in that situation was really nerve wracking because I was never sure if I was alone in the darkness.

After some searching, I finally found the generators, attached a cable, and had them hoisted.

That diving suit was never the same because the odor from the putrid water never went away.

View of Beach from Diving Barge

Fish Bombing

I had finished my repair jobs for the day and still had a craving for seafood so I went fishing as only a Navy diver could. I went to the explosives locker and got a slab of C4 explosives and a hand grenade. I unscrewed the fuse from the grenade and rolled the C4 around the detonator. I had Caddy drive our Boston Whaler skiff into the middle of the bay where I pulled the pin and threw my fishing gear as far as I could, and then we took off.

The explosion was considerably greater than I had anticipated, and the water at the center of impact rose at least three feet into the air. When the surface of the water calmed down, it was covered with all sorts of fish, some whole but dead, some just knocked out, and some already filleted. I retrieved the fish I recognized as edible and left the rest.

That night, I was able to supply the entire camp right along with a village or two in the area with enough fish for a good meal. The ferocity of the explosion convinced me that a whole slab of C4 was not necessary for fishing.

Lou in Woven Round Boat

Snaking Around

The diving barge in DaNang was extremely busy in March 1968. All sizes of boats with problems pulled up for us to perform the needed repairs. One day a MIKE boat, a flat bottom, square boat used to deliver materials and ammunition to our ports up and down the waterways of South Vietnam, came in with a bent screw (propeller). I was assigned the repair task. I rigged a nylon line from one side of the boat to the other which I could use to stand on under the boat while working. I donned a "Jack Brown" rig, a triangular mask that fit over the entire face with a surface hose for air supply and dove in to do the job.

As I worked, I noticed a shadow move behind me and realized it was a five-foot-long sea snake checking out our operations. Sea snakes are rather lethal if they sink their fangs into a person, but I decided to catch this snake for no other reason than it was there, and I could.

The diving barge had a sloping deck that ran into the water and the snake was about four feet from the slope. I swam underwater and with both hands pushed the snake onto the sloping deck. Caddy quickly got a mop and placed it on the head of the snake while another diver ran to get a bucket. We picked the snake up by the tail and placed it in the bucket where we examined and tormented it.

After a while, we decided not to let him back in the water as we were not sure of the memory capacity of a sea snake, so we called the local medevac hospital and told them we had a snake they could examine. An army ambulance soon arrived, and our poisonous friend was off on another adventure.

Mike Boat 687 with Machine Gun Mounts Made
by Lou and Caddy

Divers' Coffee Run

As part of my diving responsibilities for MCB 128, I was assigned to the diving barge in Da Nang. One day, our task was to dive into the bay to replace some underwater fuel lines that ran to the fuel depot at the air base. The fuel lines were steel pipes that went underground until they entered the water where they were replaced with rubber hoses that were coupled in thirty foot lengths.

When a fuel ship came into the bay, it would drop anchor, and personnel would radio the air base to notify them of the arrival of fuel. The crew at the air base would then pump compressed air into the hoses which made them float to the surface. The team on the fuel ship could then retrieve the hoses, bleed the air off and pump the jet fuel to the base.

There were two teams of divers, two to a team, who would do the work. This day, our skipper on the diving barge was a particularly nice warrant officer who had come through the enlisted ranks. He had been identified as officer material and given a commission.

Caddy, my diving partner, and I had finished our part of the job and returned to the diving barge in time to hear the warrant officer, Mr. F. P. Beyers, say he had run out of coffee. We noticed that a fuel ship had just come into view and had dropped anchor about two miles from our position. We told the warrant officer we could help him. We took his stainless steel thermos and jumped into the water.

Still wearing our full scuba gear, we rolled over and started to swim on our backs. The trip to the ship was quick by swimming standards since we were using UDT Duck Feet swim fins. Upon arriving at the ship, we tried to hail someone on board, but there was no answer. When the fuel ship had arrived in port, a launch had been sent to shore to pick up the mail and get some new movies, so everyone on board ship was reading mail or watching movies.

Caddy and I took off our fins and climbed up the anchor line. We began walking around the deck admiring the beautiful color scheme of the pipes. Suddenly someone from the bridge started shouting, and we were soon surrounded by crew members. I am sure that several people got bawled out that day for not noticing two people getting on board their ship in the middle of a war zone.

We told the captain of the fuel ship that we had run out of coffee and flattered him by telling him that we had heard he had the best coffee in the Navy.

He gave us two cups and filled our thermos. We were perched on the side of the ship with our swim fins on, and with a nod to each other, we fell backwards over the side.

As we swam away, we decided to give the captain a parting shot by pouring a cup of coffee into his fine china and saluting him.

We returned to our dive barge and gave the warrant officer his filled coffee container along with complimentary cups and saucers from a Navy fuel ship.

Caddy and Lou

Tug Boat at Diving Station, DaNang Vietnam

The Loss of Hanson

I first met Hanson on a job at the barge where we were working on a small boat, pulling the propeller (screw) and replacing it with a new "not bent" one. Hanson was on the "bottom," and I was tending the line. When he tugged on the line, it was supposed to be a signal for me to pull it, but I did not understand the signal so I didn't pull. Hanson erupted from the water in a rage. After a mild discussion, I apologized, and we became friends. Now, we were working together again as divers on a barge repairing boats and doing demolition jobs in DaNang, South Vietnam.

While doing this kind of work, we normally dove using a "Jack Brown" rig which was a triangular mask over the face with a surface supply air hose. A nylon line was tied around our waist to assist in bringing heavy loads to the surface. Small boats would come to the diving barge for repairs of the screws, shafts, and rudders which had been damaged by running over objects in the filthy waters.

One day, Hanson was working on a repair when someone in the boat started the engines. The boat was in gear and lurched forward. There was considerable yelling and cursing while attending divers shut the engines down.

When we tugged at the line that was tied around Hanson's waist, it was taut so we all knew there was a problem.

Several divers jumped in the water with knives in hand and swam under the boat to the place where Hanson had been working. The line tied around his waist had been caught by the shaft and wound so tightly that the loop around his waist was only inches in diameter. Hanson had been crushed to death by his safety line. No one ever admitted starting up the engines, but we had lost a diver and friend.

Our mood became very sullen and harsh. All of us were in shock. For several days no diver would go in the water, and the work began piling up.

Finally, we made a four-foot by four-foot, plywood warning sign saying there was a diver working under the boat, and the engine must not to be started. Before we would get in the water, we hung the sign in the control station of the boat on which we were to work. We, also, made an official looking document that had to be signed by the man in charge and his crew members stating that they were responsible for divers should anything happen.

Although some crew members would occasionally complain about signing the document, we never had problems again. When that happened our response was always, "You don't sign. We don't work."

After a few weeks of work on the diving barge, I would return to Camp Faulkner and MCB 128.

Diving Accident

The housing arrangements at the diving facility in DaNang were amazing. The craft on which we slept was a three- story floating motel divided into very large rooms with bunks stacked so closely together from the floor to the ceiling that there was hardly enough room to roll over.

I had been on board for about a week when I woke up one morning about 5:30 with severe stomach spasms and uncontrollable shaking. When I tried to get out of my bunk, my legs would not work, and I fell to the floor. A searing pain in my stomach kept me doubled over as I stood up and tried to make my way to the exit. Two young sailors helped me out of the barracks and along a gang plank towards the diving barge.

The lieutenant in charge did not know what was wrong but thought I might have the bends or decompression sickness, a condition caused when the nitrogen absorbed from breathing compressed air underwater remains in the body's fatty tissues and blood because of the pressure. When the pressure around the diver decreases on ascent, the nitrogen starts coming out of the tissues back into the blood stream. However, if the pressure is reduced too quickly, the nitrogen starts forming bubbles in the tissues and bloodstream rather than being exhaled, causing severe pain and sometimes death.

Although I had been diving the day before, I had only been down about seventy feet and had been careful not to stay too long. But just in case, it was decided that I should go through the procedure used in cases of the bends.

I was placed in the decompression chamber, a large steel tube shaped vessel with two lockout doors. The outside of the chamber had tubes, knobs, and various gauges that were used to pressurize the chamber to simulate a depth equivalent to one hundred seventy feet or less of sea water. I lay on a cot as the hissing of the air swirled about me until the pressure became equivalent to one hundred sixty-six feet.

I lost consciousness and was roused by a flight surgeon from the medevac hospital in Da Nang. The surgeon examined me and listened to my heart and seemed puzzled because he could not determine what was causing my shakes and pains. After a few moments, my stomach pain increased, and I again lost consciousness.

When I came to, the surgeon suggested I have some soup. It was placed in the lockout chamber and pressurized to the same level as the inner chamber, but when our door was opened, I smelled the soup and blacked out again.

The next hours were filled with severe stomach pains and episodes of blacking out and diarrhea. I was kept in the chamber all day and into the early evening as the pressure was slowly decreased in stages until it was equal to that of the surface.

When I woke up, I was in a ward filled with wounded soldiers. I had no memory of being taken from the chamber or the ambulance ride to the local medevac hospital where I had been left for care.

The ward in which I found myself was located in a Quonset hut, a long narrow tube-like building of corrugated steel with no windows and only three doors, one at each end and the third midway along the length. The nursing station was located near the midway door.

I was given a bed at the very dark, south end of the building where there were empty beds all around me. The north end was lined with the beds of the wounded. The air was permeated with the smell of plastic tubing, blood, and sweat.

I was very cold and noticed a blanket on the empty bed adjacent to mine, so I reached over to get it to cover myself. When I tucked the blanket under my chin, I felt something cold running down my neck. I lifted my hands into the dim light and saw that they were covered in blood. The blanket was soaked with the blood of a wounded soldier. I let out a cry, and the nurse was there before I could catch my breath.

Because I was an ambulatory patient, I was shown the bathroom and told to clean myself up. As I washed, my stomach pains returned with a vengeance. I ran to the commode and had ballistic diarrhea. The pain continued, and when I was able to stand, I saw the commode was filled with bright red blood. The next thing I knew I was back in bed with no knowledge of how I got there. I had a clean blanket, and the blood was gone from my bed.

While I was unconscious, the bed next to mine had been filled. I rolled over on my right side facing the north end of the ward and saw a young man who appeared to be sleeping. His head was shaved, and the right side of his skull was missing. A large scar ran into a sunken area where his brain could be seen through a thin layer of skin which was held in place by large grotesque sutures. I let out another scream, and the nurse was there again to see what was wrong.

My neighbor in the next bed was a Marine who had been on patrol and was attacked with a grenade that crushed his skull. The fragments had been surgically removed. Later when we talked, he told me that he did not care that he had been so badly hurt because he was now going home and could get a metal plate in his head to replace his skull.

It was so dark in the ward that it was difficult to distinguish night from day as there were no windows, and the doors were solid steel. Injured soldiers were continually coming in so there was seldom a lull in the activities. I was able to walk between the beds and see what the ravages of war were really like. The horrors were never ending.

One night, I woke up to hear labored breathing coming from the man in the bed across the aisle. The wounded soldier was in deep distress. At the foot of his bed was the insignia of the first air cavalry, a yellow shield with a diagonal black stripe and a silhouette of a horse head.

I got up to soothe him, and my pain put me on the floor again. When I was able to make it to his bedside, I touched his shoulder and reached over to hold his hand, trying to comfort him. His hand was coated in blood and mud, but he was not worried about his hands because he was in a struggle with the angel of death. He died as I held his hand.

I made my way back to my bed and thought about the pain that was soon to come to his family. He had a wedding ring on his left hand. How would his family deal with the sorrow of losing a loved one? Who had been praying for his safe return home?[2]

Two men went to his bed, loosened the sheets, wrapped him and carried him to the far north end of the ward, behind a screen where he was laid on the floor next to three other sheet draped comrades. The horrifying nightmare was over for these young men, but we were to endure more.

That evening there was a mortar attack, and the nurses provided us pillows to cover our heads. The pillows were little comfort because sharp flying shards of steel would not honor the barrier of a pillow.

After several days in the hospital, I was getting worse and continued to have severe diarrhea, but I was able to get up and trot to the latrine. I felt as though my insides were coming out, and the pain was so severe, it would double

[2] I later learned that the man was Richard Patrick Frasca, a twenty-six-year old counterintelligence agent from Bellport, New York.

me over. The nurses or doctors did not appear to see me as they went from one critically wounded patient to another. They had their hands full dressing wounds and changing IV bags.

I was pretty much left to myself to walk the aisle between the beds filled with the injured and watch helplessly as the ravages of war unfolded around me.

There was a very tiny Vietnamese child, a little girl about three, who sat in a makeshift crib near the nurses' station. She had been on an over-crowed bus that hit a land mine and exploded. The child lost her legs and her mother in the attack. I tried to comfort her, but she thought I was there to dress her wounds and so she began to cry.

One young man had his legs bandaged up and when they removed the bandages the flesh from his lower leg just hung detached from the bone. It was very obvious to me that he was going to lose his leg soon.

A soldier with a head injury had a tracheotomy in the base of his neck so that when he coughed, fluid would be expelled across the room.

There was an Australian soldier who was on a circular bed that rotated face up and face down. He had been shot and paralyzed from the neck down and could only scream and curse as the staff worked on him.

I was told that I would be permitted to go for meals in the mess hall some fifty yards away. I could not eat because every time I took a bite, my stomach would explode with a horrible pain that doubled me over. I was losing weight and getting weaker, but there were more critical soldiers who need the attention of the doctors.

One day as I was going to the chow hall for lunch, I became disoriented and walked the wrong way down a long walkway toward what appeared to be tents. The tents were just canvas staging areas with sawhorses and stretchers waiting for the wounded. As I turned to go back up the walkway, I heard someone scream and looked into a tent where there was a young Marine who was stripped down to his boots. He was oozing blood from a hundred small holes all over his body. His face was pocked with more holes and his eyes were gone. He told me that he had been hit with shrapnel. He was alone and in unspeakable pain. No one was there to help him.

I left the tent and started up the sidewalk going back to the ward. Until stomach pains felled me to the ground, I had thought there was a red cross on the walk to indicate a hospital. But the red turned out to be a million round circles with fine spider like projections in all directions. I realized it was blood droplets that had made the red cross. I could barely get to my feet and find my way back to my bed on the ward.

A few days later, I was transferred to the U.S.S. Repose, a hospital ship in the harbor. The Repose had been a cargo ship but because of the war, it had been converted to a hospital ship. It was old but clean. Its bright white exterior had large red crosses painted on the sides. On the top deck, there was a place for Huey helicopters to land and deposit their precious cargo of wounded soldiers.

I was assigned to a ward that had young men with minor wounds or malaria or some other infection problem. I was given IVs and fed Jell-O for days. I could get up and walk, but I had become too weak to go far and always sought the comfort of my bed.

After a week or two of constant testing, I was told that I had become infested with hookworms and two other parasites that I had gotten from the water in which I had been working. Apparently I had been cut by barnacles, and it was assumed that was where I became infected.

I was given some powerful medications that increased my diarrhea that was still bloody. My recuperation was slow. I was given small portions to eat until I could tolerate food without increasing my stomach pain.

I lost almost thirty-five pounds in one month and was very weak. I could only walk for short distances. The new uniform I was issued hung on me like a loose sack.

While I was recuperating on the Repose, I was told that I had to earn my keep by buffing floors. I had no problem buffing floors but frequently had to sit down against the walls to catch my breath.

On my second day of shining floors, I ran out of electric cord and had to find another outlet. I walked down a very tight corridor and found a socket located beside an occupied stretcher. I gave the standard greeting of "How are you feeling today?" The young Marine raised four bloody stumps and said "I can't feel a fucking thing, and I'm only nineteen years old."

I walked around the corner, leaned against the wall, and slid to the floor. What could I say? What could I do?

The evenings on the Repose were spent on the top deck which was a large open area that had been made into a movie area. Those of us who were ambulatory sat in folding chairs to watch, but there were also men in wheelchairs and on stretchers. The movies were frequently interrupted by Huey helicopters delivering more wounded on the aft deck of the ship.

One evening, the movie feature was Bonnie and Clyde. The movie was watched with half-hearted interest until sexy clips of scantily clad women would flash between scenes. Then the roar from the audience would be everything from whistles to applause.

An ironic twist was that the scene near the end of the film where Bonnie and Clyde were killed in a blaze of bullets had been edited out. The removal of the gunfire only emphasized what was happening around us.

A total of nearly six weeks passed until I was strong enough to return to my base camp in Da Nang to be reunited with my unit, but it was months before I was back to my old self.

I took a lot of kidding from the guys about having worms. They kept asking if I thought everyone should get wormed.

Navy Decompression Chamber

Blood from Above

In 1968 during the TET offensive, our battalion, MCB 128, was under lock down. No one came or went for more than a week while we guarded the perimeter to protect our turf from invasion.

The ink black sky was lit up each night with tracer rounds that made red lines from the sky to the ground. The flow of bullets was constant with tracers fired only every fifth round. Flares were in the sky continuously making eerie dancing shadows on the jungle below us. Every quadrant was lit up: North, South, East, and West.

There was a medevac hospital about a half mile north of our camp. The hueys were flying like bees. Most of the pilots had so much time at the controls that they could come in full throttle and actually stand the chopper on its tail and gently set it down on its skids.

One morning after a very long night, we were lined up in front of Company B headquarters for a head count and to receive "vital" information about the enemy. During one of the descents of a Huey, the chopper dipped and blood hit me on the left side of my face like a water balloon. I was very shocked but continued standing at attention; like a good soldier, I did not move.

When we were dismissed, I ran to the latrine where the lavatories were located. I scrubbed the now drying blood from my face and watched it swirl in the sink and wondered if it were a message from its owner, "Help me." Or was it a farewell sign?

I worried about that blood for days knowing if that quantity came from one man, it would mean his doom, and another mother dying with grief, or a father lost, or maybe a little brother confused. All for what?

Huey Medevac Helicopter

Free Helicopter Ride

When I was assigned to the command post, my work day consisted of distinct shifts, the first of which was operating the various radios and telephones in the command center, and the second was going out in the field to find and repair broken telephone lines and equipment.

One day, when I had to go to a nearby helicopter base to check on some downed lines, I learned that I could hitch a ride on a chopper just by signing in on a roster, so I signed up.

I was escorted to a very large transport helicopter with an open draw bridge in the rear. There were canvas seats lining both side and door gunners with machine guns on the right and left.

I took a seat on the left side and was soon joined by some obviously new recruits with long faces and clean new gear. The noise of the chopper was so great that it prevented conversation, so we were left to "enjoy" the ride in our own way.

The young marine sitting next to me stared silently into space for the first few minutes and then stood up and began looking out the window, watching the jungle fly by beneath us. The windows in this particular helicopter were bubbled out, and the marine found that he could rest his heavy helmet in the bubble and still see out the window.

Suddenly, I heard a scream and saw that half the marine's body was hanging outside the chopper. I jumped up, grabbed his belt, and pulled him until we both fell backwards against the opposite side of the helicopter. The window was gone and so was his helmet, but the marine was safe.

The young man crawled back to his seat, paled by the thought that he was almost introduced to the jungle in a very close-up, personal way. I was weak-kneed and anxious to get back to my base camp, away from my day of adventure.

Transport Chopper Landing

Buffalo Meat

One very hot day, I was heading South on foot looking for two broken telephone lines. I traced the wires in the sand and finally found the place where someone had cut the first line. I started to splice the wire and suddenly noticed the sand was jumping around me. Then I realized someone was shooting at me. I hit the ground and crawled into a deep ditch where I continued to splice the broken wire.

When I finished that wire, I crawled on my stomach in the ditch for about one hundred yards until I thought it was safe to get up and walk. I hadn't been shot. I didn't know if the sniper was a bad shot or just wanted to scare me, but by the time I finished, I looked like I had been mud wrestling.

I continued my repair duties and started to trace the second wire across an open field and over some barbed wire fences. I found the place where the wire had been broken by rubbing on the fence. I spliced the wire and made my way back to the main road.

I was exhausted from the heat and covered with mud from crawling on the ground earlier in the day. Since the command post was air conditioned, and the temperature there was usually in the mid-eighties during the day, it was a weclome relief to get back to the command center to have the operator check out the lines. That was much cooler and safer than the places I had been.

As I sat in the bunker trying to cool off, Lieutenant Chiomento came in to tell me where the mine fields were located. He said I would need the information before I went out on repair. The lieutenant showed me on the map that the mine fields were in the exact location where I had been working! Because it was thought impossible to walk through a mine field without being blown up, I decided that those fields were a decoy.

Two days later we learned a water buffalo had been blown to pieces after entering the very area where I had found and repaired the broken lines.

My guardian angel had been working overtime.

Water Buffalo in Vietnam

Work-A-Day

In the DaNang command post, I was in charge of the radio and telephone complex for many hours each day. When there was activity in the area, we were on high alert and constantly talking on the radios and telephones coordinating information to the perimeter of the base and to others in the area.

When there was rocket and mortar fire, the command post would fill with chain-smoking officers, which increased the tension. Commander Wittschiebe, the commanding officer, would bark out instructions for me to relay. On two occasions, I failed to use his direct quotations which made him extremely angry. Commander Wittschiebe would spin my chair around, get within inches of my face, curse, yell, and blow smoke.

I was determined to do the best I could, and according to Mr. Reardon, the man directly in charge of the unit, I was doing a fine job. After the run-ins with Wittschiebe, I decided I didn't want to work in the command center any longer so I requested a transfer to work outside in the heat with members of B Company.

Mr. Reardon, my immediate supervisor, called me in for a conference and told me if I did not withdraw the transfer request but continued to push it through, he would make sure that I did not get my next promotion. Navy promotions are based on time in rank, satisfactory completion of written study programs, and the recommendation of your immediate supervisor.

I was too stubborn to be bullied. I did not give in to Mr. Reardon and did not withdraw my request, and he did not give me a recommendation. I did not get my promotion when it was due, but I did get out of the command post.

I was upset that I was working very hard to do a good job and was punished by having my promotion blocked. I decided to act. I wrote letters to U.S. Senators from New Jersey and Delaware where I had lived, and also to Senator John Stennis, who was the head of the Senate Armed Services Committee. Senator Stennis had spoken at the recommissioning of MCB 128 in Gulfport.

I found out that the pen was as mighty as the sword when a few months later our commanding officer called for me to come to his office. I was told that if I EVER had any questions about anything that I should just let him know and for me to please stop writing letters. I never got my promotion but had some satisfaction in knowing I got my lick in.

Give Me a Break

After being released from duty in the command center at Camp Faulkner, I was assigned to B Company working on a line crew as an electrician. Our crew of eight men was assigned the task of building perimeter lighting around the Da Nang airbase ammunition dump on Hill 357.

I was working very hard with the crew setting poles and stringing lights. Since I had been in an underground bunker for months, I was not acclimated to the extreme heat and humidity.

We worked twelve hours a day every day testing the power grid, and then we ended up working a full twenty-four hours. I was so exhausted that I could hardly walk.

The evening after that twenty-four hour shift, our camp came under a mortar attack. We were just west of a small air squadron for the green berets and directly in the line of fire.

I woke up to the sirens and alerts but was too tired to get up. I decided one way or another I was going to get some rest, so I went back to sleep.

In a very short time, one of the company chiefs came in, woke me up, and started yelling. I finally got up, put on my helmet, and joined the rest of the battalion out on our perimeter. The next morning I found out that I had been written up for endangering government property.

After some thought, I devised a plan to attempt to get out of this jam. I went to the company doctor and explained the situation to him. He had gotten excellent service from me while I was in the command post, so he wrote me a fake prescription for an antihistamine that would have made me drowsy had I taken it. The prescription was backdated so that it would have been in effect just before the mortar attack.

When I presented the note to the company commander, the charge of endangering government property was dropped.

A Very Tired Lou

Hot Poles and Cold Beer

Because the ammunition facility on Hill 357 encompassed hundreds of acres, there were hundreds of poles to be set and miles of wire to string. Our job was to set telephone poles and string wires and finally to erect lighting and install transformers and switching systems to control the lights. The switches used to control the lights had to be installed in towers around the perimeter.

Our crew usually rode in a truck with an auger and winch. The holes were drilled with the auger, and we manually pushed the poles into the holes and tamped them into place. Often, the mountain slope on which we were working was so steep that the driver would have difficulty stopping at the exact location where a pole needed to be set so he would drive around until the truck slid down the hill and stopped in the right spot for the pole.

The crew climbed poles and rigged cross arms using hand tools. Bright copper wire from Canada was strung between the poles and allowed to be climatized. Because the weather was so hot, the wire would stretch and sag in one day.

While working on this project, we ran out of poles and tried, without luck, to get more. One of our supply men, who always seemed able to come up with things we needed, "acquired" some new poles. However, we soon found out that they were super creosote poles made for deep water docks.

When working on these poles, the thick toxic creosote would spew out like water from a water pistol, causing chemical burns. We were blistered from the out gushing of the harsh chemicals. Our shirtless bodies shimmered with a multicolored spectrum as the sweat captured the toxic gases being emitted from the poles.

After contemplating our predicament, we decided to tell our line chief that we needed to drink beer while working. The temperature was around one hundred ten degrees in the shade, and it was reasoned that if we drank lots of beer, we would sweat, and the sweat would protect us from the toxic gases. Our line chief thought that might work so he agreed to allow us to have beer to help "buffer" the dangerous gasses.

We decided that the beer needed to be cold, so we did what any normal bunch of Seabees would do: We devised a plan.

One of our bunch managed to steal an Air Force uniform top and a clip board. Since I had worked previously in the command center, I knew the names of all the important, high ranking officers in the area.

Early one morning, we stopped by the Air Force Enlisted Men's Club and the "uniformed" Air Force man from our crew went in carrying his clipboard. He told the men in charge of the club that the colonel, whose name I knew, needed ice every morning at 7:00 a.m. and that he would be there to get it.

Every morning on our way out to the work site, we stopped by and got ice for our beer. The ice was always ready for us without any problems, and there was plenty to cool our beer.

While we were working on a large hill around the ammo dump, we heard about the assassination of Dr. Martin Luther King, Jr. This left us all in shock and upset for a long time. We were in the land of madness. How could that madness have spilled over into the world?

Lou Up a Pole with No Place to Hide

Lou Connecting Telephone Lines

Licking and Ticking

One of the jobs we had on the line crew was erecting power lines for security lights around Hill 357 near Da Nang. Hill 357 was the main ammunition dump for the Da Nang air base, and MCB 128 was building u-shaped earthen berms to surround the munitions, bombs, rockets, and bullets stored in the open areas.

One day while we were out working, I was sent back to our base to pick up some materials that had been left behind, and I decided to take that opportunity to run by the mechanics' shed to see my diving partner, Caddy.

When I entered the shed, Caddy was just finishing up changing the oil in the rear engine of a pan earth mover with six-foot-tall tires. He was glad to see me and take a break from his work.

Caddy told me that he had broken his watchband the previous week, and his watch had fallen into a drum of old oil. He took two sticks and went over to a fifty-five gallon drum which was filled with old drain oil. After a bit of maneuvering with the sticks, he was able to retrieve his Timex watch which was fully encased in very thick, black, tar-like oil.

We took the watch out in the yard and wiped it off with a rag. Caddy then took off the back, doused it with gasoline, and set it on fire. The watched burned for three or four minutes with a rather large plume of thick black smoke.

After the watch cooled off, Caddy retrieved it, put the back on, and wound it. To my surprise, it started running. Caddy fashioned a "new" wristband out of some old tubing and was in the "time telling" business once again.

John Cameron Swayze, the newsman who starred in Timex commercials back in the "world" would have been proud since his commercials featured ways to torture Timex watches to demonstrate their toughness and reliability. Swayze's line, "They take a licking and keep on ticking," was true in the case of Caddy's watch. However, none of the Swayze commercials ever depicted the kind of treatment that Caddy's watch received.

Torture Road

While working with the crew setting telephone poles and running wire for various power distribution systems, we were given a job at the Marine Amtrak Base, located south of our base near Marble Mountain close to Da Nang. The dirt road leading to the base was the same road on which my friend, Keith McEnany, had lost his life from a land mine in October. Our whole crew was very nervous every time we approached this road ,as it was known as an enemy stronghold.

The driver of our line truck, a five thousand pound, all-wheel-drive, lumbering green machine, would stop at the beginning of the road, and we would all hang over the cab of the truck since it had sandbags in the floorboards. The driver would rev up the engine and run at top speed, often hitting bumps which caused all ten wheels to leave the ground at the same time. The theory was that if we hit a landmine it would go off behind the truck because we were moving so fast: therefore we would all make it through safely. This stomach churning activity was repeated daily for nearly two weeks until we were near the end of the job.

On the last day of our project for the Marines, we were cutting in wires to the lights around the camp. I volunteered to do the work on top of one of the poles. I climbed up the pole and drove my screwdriver into the top to attach a tagline that had a pulley and rope that was used to ferry up materials. I drilled a hole in the pole and called for a cross arm to be hoisted up and nothing happened.

When I looked down, the sight I saw wasn't good. Everyone was on the ground. Someone yelled that we were drawing sniper fire and needed to get out of there. I unbelted my climbing belt and did a combat fall, which is a free-fall almost to the ground, then digging in the climbing gear at the last minute and stepping off the pole.

The moment I started my fall, the pole was hit with sniper fire at the very spot I had been working. I got to the ground showered with splinters and rolled to the back of the truck. I hopped in, and we went roaring off to safety.

I never returned to that particular job and never got my screwdriver back.

The Remains of McEnany's Truck

Keith Allen McEnany
Panel 28E Line 61

A Different Kind of Casualty

Leonard Farabee, from Alexandria, Louisiana, was one of the first people I met when I got to Gulfport. He was sitting on a lower bunk in my cubicle the day I arrived, and we quickly became friends, going to chow hall and being on work details together. Since he was a very quiet, reserved guy, he was the one I spent lots of time with in order to stay out of trouble.

Leonard, the one who panicked during machine gun and hand grenade practice at Camp LeJeune, smoked Raleigh cigarettes just to get the coupon on the back of the pack. He always told me he was afraid to go to Vietnam because he would be killed. As time went by, he became more and more obsessed with the fear of being killed.

When we finally deployed to Vietnam and were in DaNang, Leonard was in my hooch. In a short time, he became catatonic and spent hours just standing still or sitting on his bunk without moving a muscle or saying a word. He was able to do work only if someone was with him every minute.

One Sunday morning, two naval officers came into our

hooch, and since I was in the first bunk, they asked me where Leonard Farabee was. I took them to Leonard who was sitting on his bunk just staring into space with glazed eyes.

The officers helped Leonard up to his feet, and with one officer under each arm, our comrade was escorted down the dirt road in front of our camp. We never saw Leonard again, but later discovered that he had gone insane.

The officers who lead him away never offered an explanation or took any of his personal gear. Days later when we returned from our work detail, his locker was cleaned out. Leonard was another kind of casualty that most observers of the war from afar never thought about.

Leonard M. Farabee, Jr.
12/16/1944 – 02/19/2012

Shoot It Across

We were about half finished with the job of running the power wires at the Air Force ammunition dump in DaNang when we came across an old mine field which the lines had to cross. There was no way to change the path of the wire, but none of us wanted to test our skills crossing the live field, so we had to devise a way to run the wire across.

After a few beers under the shade of our truck, we decided to try to shoot an arrow across the field. I made a bow and arrow, and we were off to the races.

The arrow was attached to a string which was attached to a light rope which was attached to the wire, then shot across. After several attempts, the wire was pulled across the mine field without any problems or casualties.

The ammunition dump power job was completed in record time, and we were all glad to have the work completed and the lights on.

Lou Working on a Communication Pole in Vietnam

Headache Below

The word of our capers spread throughout the camp, and when our safety officer heard of our activities on the line crew, he decided to give us a call. I was on the top of a thirty-five foot pole when the lieutenant came driving up in his jeep and stopped directly underneath me.

Since he did not have a real job, he started to complain to our line chief that we were not wearing our bright yellow hard hats. Now a bright yellow hard hat on top of a telephone pole in Vietnam just begs a sniper from the other team to take a shot.

After I had heard enough of his senseless orders, I decided to drop my eight-pound hammer on his jeep. My shout of "Headache" was followed by a loud bang as the hammer found its resting place in the center of the hood.

The members of the line crew all knew what "headache" meant and were prepared. For some reason, the lieutenant left in a huff and never visited us again. Message sent. Message received.

Willie Ervin from LA and Lou Drilling Water Well

Kathen Caddy Drilling for Water

Dirty Boots and New Suits

Our "homes" were called hooches. These were buildings with tin roofs, plywood on the bottom half, and screen on the upper half of the walls. The hellish heat of the day made the tin roofs concentrate the heat inside so that no living soul could stand to be in the buildings during the day. When the wind blew, the fine dirt and sand would filter through the screens and be deposited onto the waiting beds. It was so hot that the boot wax in the lockers would liquefy during the day providing us with a good excuse not to shine our boots.

One day, one of the men in the company who had just attained a new rank, decided to give our company an inspection. Now Seabees are not quick with military bearing but can get work done in impossible conditions. Without discussion, on the day of our inspection, everyone in the company fell out in the worst looking uniforms that could be found. Holes in knees, pockets torn off, and ruffled-up hats and collars were the norm.

Everyone was laughing about the members of the company being of the same mind until we noticed two hats coming our way over a rise. The brim on one of the hats had the "scrambled eggs" reserved for high ranking officers. We had not known that we were going to be inspected by the commanding officer.

The commander looked at the first three men in line and told the newly promoted man to march us down to issue to get new uniforms. We all got new uniforms, but our prank spoiled one new officer's day.

A Dirty Lou in Front of Caddy's Hooch

Destroying the Pyramids

In Vietnam, we all worked hard in the heat under difficult conditions. If we were lucky, we would get back to our base for a beer before the Enlisted Men's Club closed. The beer was always lukewarm because the coolers were overworked trying to draw the heat from the beer that had been outside all day at the supply depot.

One evening in the club, we were having a great time entertaining ourselves with a contest to determine which group could build the highest pyramids of empty beer cans on a dozen or more of the tables. Suddenly, there was a very loud noise as something came crashing through the roof. Believing it was a mortar attack, we scampered about looking like a bunch of keystone cops trying to take cover.

When the smoke cleared, we found a bag containing a spare machine gun barrel on one of the tables. That type of spare barrel was usually carried in Huey helicopters, and evidently one of the choppers had made a hard turn over our beer hall, dropping the bag, and scaring the hell out of us. The next morning the barrel was returned, with our compliments, to the local helicopter base commander.

The fear and anxiety of being in a war zone was tempered with humor and unruly behavior. Most of us were dedicated and worked as hard as possible to perform our assigned tasks the best we could. We looked after one another with respect and love, like a brotherhood. Joys and sadness were all shared in the community of the hooch, the company, and others with whom we came in contact.

Lou Doing Plumbing

The Real "Speak Easy"

Shortly after the TET offensive in 1968, our commanding officer became nervous and decided to close the enlisted men's club around eight o'clock each night in order to restrict our consumption of beer. His thinking was that we would drink so much that we would be impaired and unable to respond to an attack. Since most work crews did not get back to the base until after 6:00 p.m., the choice was whether to go to the chow hall to eat or go to the enlisted men's club and have a few warm beers. Everyone was upset that our "club" was closed, and we had no place to meet and commiserate about our miserable condition.

As usual, the men of Bravo Company came up with a solution to the problem. We built our own club house underneath Building Number 2, a hooch in our area. Every night, all the men in B Company were invited to go to Hooch Number 2 and visit the "club."

Entering the club was fairly treacherous. When one walked into Number 2, there would be a man in the second bunk on the right who appeared to be reading a book, but he was really the club guard. On the floor next to his bunk was a rug which covered a trapdoor beneath which was a narrow ladder descending into a large room some eight or ten feet in height. The room had nice tile floors and plywood walls, all constructed with materials stolen from the Air Force base. The plywood walls had been scorched with a blow torch which raised the grain of the wood, making the walls look more formal. Someone had managed to get a bunk set up. Getting the bed down the ladder and into the underground room must have been a real challenge.

The room contained a small bar and a hot plate where small burgers were sold. There was a ventilation system which exhausted the cigarette smoke and cooking odors to a location quite a distance away from the hooch.

The entire operation was surreal as we had a "limited club" that was very secret. We were able to maintain our facility and keep it in operation for nearly two months until inspection, during which the old man tripped on the rug covering the trapdoor.

The commanding officer was furious and told us to fill in the room and close the place down. We complied by pooling our money and ration cards and buying a very large amount of beer that we consumed. Then we filled in the hole by throwing the empty cans into it. This fill-in solution gave the hooch an amazing aroma for months.

Although we were very disappointed in our loss of a club, we kept smiling because we were again able to beat the system and have an opportunity to keep our sanity for a few more weeks.

Historic Pain

After being transferred from the command post in DaNang, I was assigned to several work details including a line crew. The line crew would work on electrical power distribution systems and the wiring of buildings for various military bases in the DaNang area.

One day after I had finished work, our five-ton transport truck came along to give me a ride back to the base. I joined other electrical crew members and the plumbers on the back of the truck. One person who was in that group was St. Germain, a Native American from the Sioux Nation. St. Germain was always drunk and very sullen, but since we had shared the same barracks back in Gulfport, we had a good relationship. His only reason for being in Vietnam was that he believed it was better than being on the reservation.

I noticed that St. Germain had saved a can of fruit cocktail from his lunch C-rations. As the truck bounced at breakneck speed down the road toward the base, we spotted two small children walking on the side of the road. A small young boy about seven years old and his big sister were no doubt walking home. As we approached the pair, St. Germain threw his can of fruit cocktail and hit the small boy in the back of the head. I turned to see the child sprawled out on the ground with his sister bending over him. I was horrified.

St. Germain had hit his target, but there was no emotion on his face.

I have thought about that small boy over the years and wondered what happened to him. Does he have vision problems or perhaps constant headaches from the severe blow to the back of his still developing skull? What did his parents do? What did they say? How did they cope with the terror imposed by those who supposedly were there to help?

I wanted to grab St. Germain and shake him. I wanted to stop the truck, but we were moving too fast. I felt helpless and ashamed at this unabashed act of cruelty. I wanted to ask St. Germain why he felt compelled to hurt an inno-cent child, but I knew that he, too, had been hurt as a child.

St. Germain carried the pain of a nation on his shoulders, and his way of coping with it was to continually drink and lash out as he did by throwing that can at a helpless child. How deep was the pain in his heart? How miserable he had to be to sacrifice himself to the cause of Viet-namese when he had not been required to do so.

I have never forgotten the pain of St. Germain or the pain of that unfortunate young child. I pray that both have somehow found peace in their lives.

Signs of the Time

Bravo Company consisted of electricians and plumbers. The company shop was a large metal building that was divided in half with the electricians on the north end and the plumbers on the south end.

The electricians decided to make a sign to mark their location in a fun sort of way. On a four-by-eight-foot sheet of plywood, one of the men drew a Charlie Brown wearing a barrel and suspenders. Under the picture were the words, "We Remove Your Shorts, B Company MCB 128."

Not wanting to be outdone, the plumbers got a piece of plywood exactly like the electricians' and wrote the words "Remember, Your Shit is Our Bread and Butter, B Company MCB 128." Pictured on that sign was a slice of toast spread with a dark, apple butter consistency substance with flies circling around it.

The officers in charge did not appreciate the humor and promptly ordered the signs be taken down. The morale suffered because humor and one-upmanship helped give us the determination to survive.

123

WE REMOVE
YOUR SHORTS

B COMPANY
MCB 128

Mail Call

Officer Chiomento, the security officer who was responsible for having the electricians and plumbers remove their signs, noticed that the company mailroom had open mailboxes which were labeled A though Z. The company clerk would sort the mail as it came in and place it alphabetically by surname in the boxes so that we could pick up our mail whenever we had an opportunity.

Officer Chiomento decided that the arrangement for our getting mail was not acceptable since it was not secure so he had a front made for the boxes and posted mail hours. When the work crews came in, no one could get any mail since the hours the boxes were open were not compatible with the work schedules. As the crews came in from work, more and more men gathered in disbelief that the mail had been locked up. The room was soon completely full of angry Seabees.

When Okerstrom, a muscular, six-foot-three electrician, came in and saw what had happened, he became uncontrollably angry. He quickly left the room and came back with two sledge hammers. Everyone stepped aside to give him plenty of space while he made splinters of the new door over the mailboxes. Everyone then took turns smashing the box until there was not enough left to be held in our hands.

Nothing was ever said about the incident, but after that day, we all found our mail on the counter in the mailroom.

Military Payment Certificates
Issued by the U.S. Government
to American Soldiers in Vietnam

The Trash Man Runneth

Although the Bravo Company to which I was assigned was made up of plumbers and electricians, and I was an electrician, I was temporarily assigned to be the trash man. I drove a five-ton dump truck around our base picking up trash from the cans and central supply.

One day late into the morning run, I was assigned a new helper. I parked the truck on the only hill in the camp, killed the engine and let truck roll backward. I popped the clutch with the truck in first gear and set the brake after putting the truck in neutral. I found my new helper at the bottom of the hill and asked him to go up and get the truck which was still running. He gladly ran off to get the truck, excited about being allowed to drive.

He got in the truck and put it in first gear, let the clutch out, and the truck lurched backward. Second gear and again the truck roared in reverse. Finally, the newcomer put the truck in reverse, and the truck sprang forward.

The engine was racing when he finally got to the bottom of the hill. I yelled at him for not knowing how to drive a truck. I turned the engine off and continued to lecture him about the instructions on the dash of the truck. I started the truck and demonstrated that first gear made the truck go forward as did second and third, while reverse caused the truck to back up.

I do not know if every multi-fuel truck in the armed forces had an engine that turned over backwards, but this truck sure did. I never explained to my new helper about the gears, but others in B Company learned the trick with the trash truck.

South Vietnamese Money

TET Phone Repair

A few minutes after midnight on January 30, 1968, all hell broke loose. The TET offensive had begun. We were all awakened by loud explosions and small arms fire. Our battalion of about nine hundred men was instructed to move quickly to defend the perimeter of our base in order to protect our "home" from the advancing Viet Cong and North Vietnamese Army.

Each company of the battalion was assigned an area to protect using a string of fighting holes interspersed with bunkers. Communication was maintained between the large bunkers and the command center in the heart of our camp. Minutes ran into hours, and the tension was horrendous as we sat and waited for something to happen, all the while praying that nothing would.

The Company B commander came around to our fighting hole to see me. The communication wires between two of the main bunkers had gone down, and he wanted me to fix the problem. I had been known as the "can do" kid ever since my diving training, so I was the one usually selected for this kind of assignment.

I quickly got my tool pouch and extra combat communication wire and started crawling around the perimeter of the base to seek out the broken wire. I was very concerned with this new assignment because I was crawling directly between my comrades-in-arms and the enemy.

I pulled the wire up through the hot sand as I crawled along tracing the wire from the first bunker to the front of the second bunker. I was as flat as I could possibly be and was about fifteen feet from the base of the second bunker when all of a sudden someone in the bunker started firing an M-60 machine gun directly over my head. My heart nearly stopped from fright, but somehow I managed to get up to the base of the bunker and yell out, "Hold your fire. I am out here working on the telephone."

The screams and commotion inside the bunker was heard all around the perimeter. I finally calmed down enough to go inside where I found that someone had stepped on the wire to the phone which caused it to be disconnected. When I finished the repair job, I rejoined my company in the fighting hole. I had not been shot, but I felt like I had lost ten years of my life from the scare.

Mosquito Repellent

The whole ordeal of the constant attacks during the TET offensive lasted nearly a week at our location, and our battalion was locked down inside our small camp. We all rotated from the perimeter to inside the camp for showers, changes of clothes, and rations. There was never true rest because of the continuous noise of fighting all around.

The second night of the attack on the base, I spent out in the fighting hole. It was a little chilly so I slipped on a camouflage nylon type poncho liner that was a cover for use in cold weather.

Just before putting on the liner, I had put on military issue mosquito repellant to keep the ever present mosquitoes at bay. Soon the poncho liner began to dissolve. The chemicals in the mosquito repellent were strong enough to melt the fabric in my source of warmth. After that I decided it was better to stay awake and warm and swat mosquitos than to use the military issue bug repellent.

Lou Getting Ready for Guard Duty

Not Their Son

I had just come home on leave from my first tour of duty in Vietnam and was in shock when I realized where I had been and what I had seen. Now I was finally in the work-a-day world of home where things were humming along, not missing a beat. People did not seem to be bothered by what was happening on the other side of the world. Vietnam might as well have been on another planet. This powerful impression kept me out of step with the people around me. This time was very uncomfortable for me, even if I was on leave.

My parents had moved shortly after I joined the Navy and left for basic training at Great Lakes Naval Station. I did not know a single person in the new town.

My mother must have sensed my discomfort and decided to include me in her daily activities of cleaning and grocery shopping. One day, she decided to send me to the grocery store for some milk and bread. When I got into her car, an old mint green Studebaker Lark, I noticed a Seabee sticker on the rear bumper. I had sent it to my little brothers from Vietnam along with other things they might like to have from a foreign county.

As I drove the five miles to a local shopping center, I noticed I was being followed. When I came out of the grocery store, a man who was waiting by my car, begged me to follow him home for just a minute. He said his son was in the Seabees, and he wanted his wife to meet me. I agreed and with some hesitation followed the man to his home. We drove a short distance from the shopping center to a neat middle-class housing development.

By the time I got the car parked, the man came rushing up to the curb from his driveway to help me get out. He was obviously very excited and could hardly wait for us to get in his house. Before I knew what was happening, I was standing in the middle of a modest kitchen with the man, his wife, and his daughter.

The wife escorted me to the dining room as the man dashed madly around the house gathering pictures of a boy in a baseball uniform and a scout uniform. It was apparent that this was an all-American family justly proud of their son. The man and his wife were in a frenzied state telling me about their Seabee son, and wanted to know if I knew him. The commotion finally stopped, and the family began crying as the man confessed that their son[3] had been killed in Vietnam.

We all stood around the table crying for what seemed like hours. I realized that they were wishing beyond reason that I would be able to say that I knew their son, that there had been a terrible mistake and he was alive and would be home any day, just as I was there with them.

---

[3] Jon James Hayden, MCB 11, Equipment Operator, 12/15/1946-8/16/1967, Wall Panel 24E, Line 116

I do not know or remember how or when I left their home that day. I never saw them again, but I carried their pain for years, wondering how they were coping. It stirred within me such deep feelings of anger, fear, and sorrow that I will never forget the family and the pain they suffered.

Studebaker like my Mother's Car

Seabees Bumper Sticker

Please Believe Me

While home on leave, after my first tour of duty in Vietnam, I realized I did not know a single person in my parents' new home town. I decided to borrow my father's car and visit my sister in New Jersey.

While in New Jersey, I took my aunt, who was special to me, out to eat. I did it up right by wearing a suit and taking her to an upscale eating establishment.

The following evening, I decided I would drive to Burlington, New Jersey, where my former girlfriend lived. This girlfriend had sent me a "Dear John" letter while I was away in training in preparation to deploy. I was unsure and uncomfortable about the visit because I did not want to make trouble in the event she had a new gentleman friend.

I drove by her house but didn't have the courage to stop, so I went on by and turned around in a furniture parking lot and went back toward her house. By that time, I had gotten my nerve up and was determined to knock on her door.

I was about four blocks away from her house when all of

a sudden three police cars with their sirens blaring and lights flashing surrounded my car and pulled me over. As the policemen got out of their vehicles, I immediately noticed that they were all squatting behind the doors of the squad cars with their guns drawn, and I was their target.

I was told by a policeman using a loud speaker to get out of the car and place my hands on the roof which I did quickly. I always followed orders. The policemen came up, shoved me around, and asked for my driver's license.

I reached for the license, and it was not in my pocket. I had left it in my suit pocket after taking my aunt to dinner the previous night.

The police tore my dad's car apart searching it. They told me a bank had been robbed, and the car I was driving matched the description of the getaway car.

I told them who I was and then remembered that one of my neighbors in Riverside was a policeman who knew me and my family. I gave them his name, and they radioed for verification.

After he vouched for me, the police were satisfied I was not their man. They turned their lights off and went on their way, leaving me to put my father's car back together, back seat, trunk, tool box, glove box, and all.

While I was working, I was carefully watched by several people standing on their porches and in their driveways. I waved to the bystanders as I got in the car, but strangely none of them waved back.

I decided to go back to my sister's house and then on back to Delaware. I was ready to get out of town and never had the opportunity to call on my old girlfriend. I didn't have the desire to be in that neighborhood again.

Lou at Home Wearing his Suit

Caddy and Lou

Surviving Survival Training

Near the end of my first tour of duty in Vietnam, a memo had been sent out to the battalion asking for volunteers to work for the U. S. State Department on their second tour in country. We all knew that we were going to come back since there were not enough Seabees in the military, so I decided to take the bait and go for the adventure. I signed up with the officer in charge and was told that I would start training as soon as I got back to Gulfport, Mississippi.

After returning to the United States and a short rest at my parents' home, I began training with our designated unit, MCB 12801. There were thirteen of us in the team, a junior grade lieutenant, a chief petty officer, and eleven of us peons. We were to be cross-trained so we could survive if one of our team members were injured or could not perform his duties.

We had lessons on the cultural norms of the Vietnamese people. We were sent to Los Angeles to Vietnamese language school, which involved intense mind-numbing sessions that were ten hours a day for twenty-one days.

Louis Remmers

We attended classes in welding, steel cutting, general construction, and wood and concrete work. We were trained to operate bulldozers, road graders, and front-end loaders and were lectured on a variety of weapons such as machine guns, mortars, and hand grenades. Some of the weapons discussed were from World War II.

In September 1968, we were flown to Maine for survival training school. The majority of those who were being trained were pilots, since if they were shot down in enemy territory, they would most likely to be on their own and need to know how to survive until rescued.

There were sixty men in our training group. We were divided up into ten-man teams and bussed into the wilderness of northwestern Maine where we were ushered into a large tent filled with wooden benches. Standing at the front of the room were three instructors who demonstrated the way to kill and skin a rabbit and prepare it to be eaten.

After killing and skinning the rabbit, an instructor asked for a volunteer from our group to show the rest of us how he would do it. One young Navy Seal came forward from the back of the room, took one of the rabbits, bit it in the throat to kill it, and promptly skinned the little critter.

When this lesson was complete, three rabbits were distributed to the sixty men. The rabbits were then killed and distributed among the teams. This came out to one-half rabbit for every ten men. Slim rations, but that was the point.

My ten-man team boiled our half rabbit in an old steel helmet and felt lucky that we were given the head instead of the internal organs. After eating the rabbit broth, each of us sacked out with the blanket that he had been issued.

The next morning, each of us was given a map, a compass, and a small Frosted Flake looking food bar and told to find our way to a designated checkpoint. We were told to run for our lives because we would be pursued by "armed enemy combatants." Anyone captured would be taken to the local POW camp.

There were two choices: find the easiest route or find the hardest. I decided that I needed to go on the most difficult terrain available in order to evade the enemy. I wanted to make it rough for the individuals who were trying to capture me.

I found a very grueling route along a steep ridgeline on the side of a mountain. On the far side of the ridgeline was Canada. The next road was about three hundred miles northwest of my position. I ate mountain clover and small trees along with a few bugs and drank from mountain streams to keep hydrated. I tried to catch some badly need sleep by spending nights up in trees or under rocks and fallen trees and brush.

For a while, I had a companion, a corpsman from my sister unit MCB 12802, but he decided the going was too rough, so he went down the mountain where he was soon captured and taken away. From a safe distance, I witnessed several of my fellow trainees being seized by the men in black and taken away to the POW camp.

I finally made it to the designated check point and was picked up by "friendly forces," and taken to an old run-down mobile home that was full of bunks. I was given a bologna sandwich on stale bread, which at the time I thought tasted better than any steak I had ever eaten.

There were only ten of us out of the original sixty who had been able to escape the enemy and make it to safety. We were allowed to sleep for five hours, and we took full advantage of that opportunity.

The next morning, we were given two cups of coffee and told to form up outside the trailer. We were marched three miles down a dirt road to the POW camp, a compound surrounded by a large barbed-wire fence with guard towers around the perimeter.

We were immediately greeted by very big guards dressed in black uniforms and speaking with phony foreign accents. They seemed glad to see us since we were the prime nuts to crack.

One at a time, we were roughly escorted into a very small room with mirrors lining the back wall. We were badgered and pushed and thrown against the walls to soften us up.

I decided that I was tough because I had completed diving training and was in rather good condition, so my responses to the questioning were "John Wayne" in nature. This exacted a heavy price in pain and infuriated my captor, who called in a friend who was large enough to block out the light in the doorway as he entered the room.

"Igor's" greeting began with a slap across my face that knocked me to the floor. I had his hand print from the crown of my head to my chin. I soon realized that the "John Wayne" persona was for the movies, and I had better cooperate. I asked my interrogator what he wanted, and he told me to crawl out of the room on my hands and knees, which I gladly did without saying a word.

The POW experience only lasted three or four days, but it seemed much longer. Even now, it is a blur. We were finally liberated in very patriotic fashion, and that ordeal was over.

Most of us were bussed backed to the main base, but a few men were taken to the hospital. The following days were spent in debriefing to help us understand how we reacted and how we should have reacted. This retrospective study gave insight into the treatment of POWs. All of us agreed that we did not want to be taken captive in Vietnam.

Machine Gun Training

Requalification for Diving

Our leave time was over, and Caddy and I were again in Gulfport, Mississippi, training for a second tour. Caddy had spent his leave in Massachusetts and returned to Gulfport driving an Oldsmobile Vista Cruiser station wagon. Most twenty-or-so-year-olds would not want to drive a station wagon, but it suited us just fine since it provided space for all of our toys.

About the time we were beginning training, we got orders to go to Panama City, Florida, for our requalification dives. The requalification dives were scheduled every six months, but in reality they were designed to get some work done in the water. We drove the Vista Cruiser from Gulfport on old Highway 90 to Mobile and then on to Panama City, Florida.

Upon arrival, we were delighted with the small Navy base that was an underwater mine defense base for Navy mine sweepers. We had deluxe accommodations in a barracks that gave us a room to share.

On our first day, we were given dive bags that contained all of the gear to be used and a huge bottle of Coppertone suntan lotion. We were immediately scheduled to go out to a platform about five miles off shore and were told to go to the mess hall to pick up box lunches to take to the crew.

The boat that took us to the platform was a very slow cabin cruiser, the kind that the civilians used for pleasure. We were a bit confused. Our chief in charge told us it was a way to relax and still do our work so we fell right in line. It took a long time to get out to the platform, so we enjoyed sunbathing on the front deck of the boat.

When we reached the platform, we were surprised to see a three-story building on stilts in about one hundred fifty feet of water.

Our job was to take electronic equipment down to a capsule in one hundred feet of water. The capsule was being prepared for a sea lab project to see how humans would adapt to undersea conditions for extended periods of time.

Caddy and I were the first dive team to go over the side. Our bottom time passed quickly, and we went to the surface to send the next team down to finish the job.

Since Caddy and I were both a little hyper, we decided to snorkel and see if we could spear some fish. We had one Hawaiian gig, which was a long stainless pole with a frog gig on the end and elastic tubing on the other end. It was very effective at close range.

Caddy had first dibs on the gig, so he told me to float on the surface to see if any fish would come take a look. I did as he instructed and was thrown against the leg of the platform's stage by a rogue wave. My back instantly started burning, and I swam over to Caddy to have him take a look. He inspected my injury and said everything was fine, so we resumed hunting.

Suddenly we noticed there was a very large school of barracuda encircling us so we decided to go for one with the gig. The fish was injured and started slowly swimming on its side. We followed. He kept swimming, and we kept following him deeper and deeper, wearing only snorkel gear until I noticed my depth gauge indicated we were at one hundred feet. My chest was really hurting, so I signaled Caddy, and we returned to the surface for a deep breath of air.

We lost the injured fish but managed to spear another barracuda and took it to the boat. We later got a small shark and were ready to go back for more when we saw Momma coming around our boat. The momma shark was about ten feet long and our Hawaiian gig was no match for her.

We started the trip back to the base and resumed our sunbathing on deck when I noticed I could not get out of my chair because of dried blood. Caddy said the cut was from barnacles, and my heavy bleeding had helped draw a shark or two.

Our time at the Panama City base seemed more like a vacation than work, testing underwater equipment for which the Navy was considering giving contracts. We had our choice of mini-subs, special gear, and all sorts of secret new inventions.

One afternoon, our officer in charge got a call from the sheriff in Port St. Joe, Florida, requesting divers to assist in searching for the body of a drowning victim. Caddy and I were selected for the job, and we, along with our

Louis Remmers

gear, were driven to Port St. Joe in the back of a Navy pickup truck and taken to a sand dredge near a river.

Some little boys had been swimming, and one had gone under and never come up. The area of the search was a sand bluff with a small, moving, river-like body of water some twenty feet deep. There was already a tent set up for the family, and it was filled with black people crying and trying to console one another.

Caddy and I immediately went to work in a circular dive pattern to cover as much of the bottom as possible. The current was swift, and visibility was less than two feet. After working for about two hours, we changed our search pattern and began swimming from bank to bank across the current using a rope to guide us.

On one trip, I came up at the back of an aluminum boat with the sheriff in the stern. The sheriff was like a character out of a movie: over three hundred pounds in khaki uniform with a cowboy hat and mirrored sun glasses. He was getting tired of waiting and was sweating profusely. He leaned over to me and told me to wrap it up, but to put on a good show as he motioned his head to the family in the tent. He then said, "Heck, it's only a little nigger boy, and as hot as it is, he will pop up like a fishing cork in a few days."

I was shocked and angered to think he could be so callous towards a little boy. I thought of all the times when I was growing up and took chances swimming in less than safe areas. I could have been the one popping up like a fishing cork.

150

We did wrap it up after concluding the current was so swift the body could be anywhere downstream in a hollow on the bottom.

Afterwards, the sheriff took us to a local restaurant that had already closed to the general public, fed us steaks, and offered to put us up for the night. Before that offer, I had decided that I wanted to get away from that "so-called" lawman as soon as I finished eating, so we declined his offer. We had a very cool ride back to the base that night, and I thought about the family of that little boy.

We spent another week in Panama City, diving and improving our tans.

On the last day, we managed to get another barracuda which we brought back on the boat. Since it had not been refrigerated, it was very stiff by the time the boat came in.

We saw our chief who had been having a few drinks and told him he could have the barracuda, and that it was great to eat. He took it and put it in the trunk of his new black Chevy convertible.

We left the base that same day and headed back to Gulfport to resume training for our next tour of duty.

During this time when Caddy and I were in Gulfport between deployments, we had lots of time to spare and spent most of it hanging out and enjoying the break. We often visited Mike Johnson, a friend of Caddy's from A company. Mike, who was from Bath, Maine, had just gotten married, and he and his wife were living in Kim K Apartments which were off base, just south of the main gate of the Seabees base.

One Saturday, Caddy and I decided to go swimming and went over to Mike's to see if he and his new wife wanted to go. As we were walking up to Mike's apartment, we noticed two nice-looking young ladies sitting on one of the balconies at the end of the complex. We went on to Mike's and convinced him and his wife to go, but we couldn't forget the girls we had seen earlier. As we were leaving, Caddy and I decided to ask them if they would go swimming with us.

By that time, they had gone inside so we knocked on their door. One of the girls, whose name was Linda, answered, and we asked, "Wanna go swimming?" Linda answered, "No, I don't even know you," so we introduced ourselves. However, our offer was still declined.

Caddy and I kept going back to visit Mike and his wife and eventually got dinner dates with the two young ladies who were in their final year of training as medical technologists. They were students at the University of Southern Mississippi and were on the coast doing clinical training at the Gulfport Memorial Hospital. From that time until I left for my second tour, I saw lots of Linda.

Before his deployment, a friend gave me a 1960 Corvair that I gave to Linda for safe keeping. She and her roommate could use the car while I was gone to Nam, and it would give me a good excuse to stay in touch.

At Christmas I took leave to visit my family in Delaware. I left Delaware after church on Christmas day, flew to

Gulfport and left there the day after Christmas for Vietnam for the second tour.

This time I was part of a thirteen-man civic action team, MCB 12801, assigned to a small village about a two hours' drive north of Saigon. Thu Duc was to be our home for the next year.

Lou with his Barracuda

The Thirteen-Man Crew from MCB 12801

*Front Row (L to R): J. Emory, B. Hinds, J. Roberts, R. Hawes,
C. Mestayer, J.C. Tanner*
*Second Row (L to R): Lt. Tway, G. Dowdy, D. Carney, L. Remmers,
P. Wharen, J. Yost, D. Pryor*

Clean Clothes

During my second tour of duty, we worked on counter insurgency around the small village of Thu Duc. We built bridges, schools, and roads to help the people and let them know we were really not that bad.

Our officer in charge was a junior grade officer who decided that we needed to work more with the villagers in buying supplies and the like. We purchased food from the local market and endured the diarrhea for months until we became acclimated to the food.

We were instructed to allow a local to wash our uniforms, so we complied. After a few weeks, I developed some very large sores on my back. The sores grew to the size of baseballs, making it difficult for me to walk and sleep.

Our corpsman decided to get me some help so we loaded up one day, and he drove me to Long Binh, a large army base in V corps in the southern part of South Vietnam.

We were fortunate to be able to see a physician who was a dermatologist. He had me lie down and proceeded to stab the sores with a scalpel. Not wasting time with any anesthesia, the doctor just stabbed and squeezed the sores. I decided that after six stabbings, I had had enough and got off of the table.

I was taken back to our camp and decided I could fix my own problem. I rigged a hot water heater and heated water to near scalding. I soaked a towel in the hot water and placed it on my back. Several agonizing days later, the sores were gone and I was able to return to normal activities.

I decided to go see where our "laundry man" had his shop and found it located at the bottom of a hill with a catch basin to catch rain water from the village. When it rained, the village people would place trash including feces in the road where the rainwater would sweep it away. The catch basin for the laundry was the repository of all the village refuse, and we were wearing it on our backs.

From that time on, since I never had enough time to build a washing machine, I decided to hand wash my own clothes.

Outhouse over Fishpond

Give Me My Rights

One day, Paul Wharen, the "supply" man in our small unit was arrested by the MPs while he was talking with some of the Vietnamese. He was taken to Long Binh jail which was a large shipping container with slots cut in it to form jail house bars. The MPs, not knowing of Paul's status as a State Department representative, were going to throw the book at him, but he had other ideas.

After being in the hot box for a while, Paul started making lots of noise. He told his captors that according to the Geneva Convention he was entitled to an exercise period. The MPs not knowing what to do, granted him time to get out of the box to do jumping jacks and jog in place. The MPs were not up on the Geneva Convention. Since any soldier who was arrested would lose rank and beg for mercy, they were not accustomed to anyone demanding rights.

Next, Paul banged on the shipping box and demanded water. The MPs accommodated him.

Paul's final defiant act was when he asked for his free phone call. They were shocked, and not being sure, granted him a free call.

Who are you going to call in Vietnam? Paul asked for a phone book and was given a list of names. A general in Saigon caught his eye, so he called the general. It just so happened that this general was connected with the State Department and promptly chewed out the main MP. The general told the MP to give Paul Warren anything he wanted.

Paul had the MPs wash his jeep and have the chow hall opened up so he could have a steak. They had to comply, and once again, that bunch of MPs was glad to see this wayward soul get out of their sight.

Paul Wharen
The "Supply Man" Who Knew How to Find it and Get it

Generator Problems

Each morning while shaving, my eyes focus on the scar on the bridge of my nose. I am immediately taken back to the events that created that small scar and reminded how lucky I am to be alive.

I was on my second tour of duty in Vietnam, assigned with a team of thirteen men to a small outpost in a village north of Saigon called Thu Duc. I was the electrician in charge of providing the electrical needs of our camp. Our electricity came from an Onan generator that ran twenty-four hours a day, seven days a week and had been doing so for years. The generator was worn out long before we arrived and had the equivalent of at least three hundred thousand car miles.

Not too long after my arrival at Thu Duc, I was suddenly awakened in the middle of the night by a sound that just wasn't right. The hum of our old generator had changed pitch, a clear sign that there was trouble on the way.

I went to the generator and tried to pet it as best I could, but it was old and tired and in the inky blackness of night, it was running full speed trying to keep up with the power demand of our compound.

A few days earlier, I had run a wire from our camp to a small, nearby refugee camp so the children there could watch the television station that was broadcast in country by the U.S. military. Most of the programming was for U. S. soldiers, but there were some Vietnamese programs in the early evening.

The morning after the problem with the generator, I investigated and discovered that some of the refugees had hot-wired off my wire and were trying to run all sorts of devices.

The old Onan generator had three wiring sections that produced current as the main shaft rotated around the center. It was important to balance the loads to evenly distribute the work between the three wirings. The Vietnamese who hot-wired on my circuit were over drawing, and the generator had to strain to carry the heavy load it was turning. I had no choice but to disconnect the wire to the refugee camp.

The night after I disconnected the electricity, our camp came under fire from small arms and explosives. Our team quickly ran out into the perimeter fighting holes and prepared for the worst. There was a loud sound, and I found myself on my back with my face covered with blood. I had been hit with something, probably in retaliation for disconnecting the electrical service.

I was unhappy that I could not give the refugee children some evening entertainment, so several days later I discussed the problem with my commanding officer, Lieutenant John Tway. He contacted some officials from the U.S. State Department who were our direct contacts in country. Days later, a package of documents arrived for us to complete by telling what was wrong with the generator we had, its age, and why we needed a new one. A week later we were contacted and told to go to Saigon to get a new generator. Dan Carney, one of the mechanics, and I were sent in a dump truck to pick up the geneator and bring it back to our base.

Now "Dan the Mechanic" was a big fan of the then new NASCAR races, and he along with another mechanic, Jim Youst, had souped-up our truck. They had managed to reconfigure the engine and take the governor off, making the truck run about as fast as a race car.

We were tooling along on Long Binh Highway far beyond the capabilities of the truck's speedometer when we heard a siren coming from an MP jeep that was on our tail. We finally stopped and were approached by two Army MPs, one of whom had a ticket book in his hands. He was poised to give us a speeding ticket.

In the military, the consequence for receiving a ticket was getting busted and losing rank, so it was normal to plead for mercy. However, since we were assigned to the U. S. State Department and on "loan" to the U.S. Navy Seabees, we were not the norm; we didn't need to plead for mercy.

First the Army MPs started to harass me for not wearing a hat to which I replied that we had been going so fast that it had blown out the window.

We continued to counter their questions with wild unbelievable answers until one said we were going to see the

Provost Marshal, the most senior MP in the area. I turned
to Dan and said, "Did you hear that? Marshal Provost is
back in country."

That did it. The MPs realized that we were not right
somehow, so they radioed for back up. In almost no time,
there were three jeeps and six MPs surrounding our truck.

After finding out who we were, the sergeant asked us to
please leave and stop bothering his MPs. We gladly
granted his wishes and mounted our trusty NASCAR
dump truck, leaving the MP crew standing in a cloud of
black smoke.

We proceeded on to Saigon where we found the generator
waiting at the dock near the main river. After signing a
dozen papers, we were on our way with our brand new
generator, manufactured in Pittsburg, Pennsylvania. We
returned back to our small camp before nightfall, which
was our intention in the first place.

By the next afternoon, I had made all the connections for
the power cables, buss bars, and fuel supply lines, and the
new unit was up and working. Just six hours later, again
in the middle of the night, the sound of the new generator
increased in tone, indicating that it too had lost its load.

I worked for three hours in the hot, dark generator shed
trying to figure out what was wrong. My only source of
illumination was a lone flashlight. The new generator
could not produce power. I started the old Onan and went
back to bed until daylight.

The next morning, I inspected the new generator and found that the electronic circuit was fried from a small nut and washer falling onto the circuit. The generator was a three-cylinder diesel that was not very well balanced causing it to vibrate terribly. The vibrations loosened the nut causing it to fall off and into the delicate electrical excited circuits.

I made repairs and was able through some miracle to get the new generator online again, but just twelve hours later, it happened again and this time it was only 11:00 p.m. Over the next three weeks, I battled with the new generator until I finally surrendered. I didn't have any replacement parts left so I was finished with the generator.

Our nighttime security depended on my ability to keep the generators running so that the perimeter of the camp could remain lit. I was really down knowing that I had to try to keep two bad generators running.

We were relatively isolated without a normal supply network so we secured what we needed from the local village. Anything we were unable to obtain locally, our "acquisition man" in the field, Paul Wharen, was usually able to find.

Paul slept in the bunk next to mine, and I disturbed his sleep by constantly getting up to check on the generators. Since we were assigned to the U. S. State Department, we had little military support, but Paul was great at "acquiring" what we needed. Paul decided to take matters into his own hands and told me that he had a surprise for me.

The following Sunday afternoon, Paul informed me and four more of the men that we were going for a ride in the country. The four of us hopped into a small weapons carrier, a military version of a pickup truck with a tent on the back, and headed for an army post called Long Binh, a tent city north of Saigon. Paul had scouted out a whole field of generators on trailers in a large compound.

Once on the army post, Paul drove to an open area that had about two acres filled with army generators on trailers. The army had just begun to ring the area with barbed wire. While the rest of us stood on the fence to depress it, Paul drove over it in the weps. Then Paul told me, "Pick one out, and I'll buy it for you."

I went from generator to generator firing them up and looking at gauges until I found one I liked. We hitched the trailer which held that generator up to the back of our little truck and off we went through the back roads of the post toward the rear gate.

On the way, Paul opened a stick of Doublemint gum and began to chew. Then he folded the silver wrapper and attached it to his collar with the chewing gum. He now had a field commission and instantly became a Lieutenant in the army.

As Paul drove through the back gate without slowing down, the private on guard duty gave him a snappy salute. That generator saved our lives, and I still chew Doublemint gum.

Vibrating Generator from Saigon

The Pittsburg Generator

Downtown Saigon

A Broken Rifle

While stationed in the small camp in Thu Duc, South Vietnam, one of our crew came under sniper attack while he was driving a bulldozer. He quickly jumped from the dozer while trying to hold on to his rifle. As he made his exit, he dropped his rifle, and it was run over by the moving dozer. The weapon was then useless and could not be fired. It would have to be replaced.

My diving partner, Kathen Caddy, and I had been separated, and he was still in the main battalion in Quang Tri while I was with the Seabees Team 12801 in the South. I had been wanting to go visit him in the North, and a trip to take the damaged rifle and swap it for a working one gave me that opportunity. I quickly volunteered to take the rifle to Quang Tri to get a replacement. I was excited about the trip because it would give me a break from the hard work and a chance to visit with Caddy.

I flew by C130 fixed wing and then by helicopter to the base at Quang Tri. I was instructed to first return the rifle and get a new issue, so I looked up the supply officer whom I had known from my first tour in Vietnam. All of the officers I knew were very glad to see me, and we had a great mini reunion.

My friends there decided that I should play a practical joke on a security officer that they didn't like. This security officer was a "Frank Burns" by the book type. I was to be the "Sad Sack" and was able to play the part well since my uniform was soiled, and my boots were not shined.

I stood at attention while the officer in question came into the room. He barked an order to present arms which was a signal for me to hold the weapon in a manner that he could take it from me. I snapped the gun in position, and as he grabbed it from me, it fell apart in his hands, pinching his fingers. I could hear the sound coming from the next room as his fellow officers laughed about having pulled a good joke on him. He could do nothing about it as I was a State Department employee at the time. I was issued a new rifle in the appropriate owner's name (not mine) and was quickly off to see Caddy.

I went to the mechanics and repair shop to find him but did not see him, so I had to ask. The reply was that Caddy was a little unruly and was assigned to fix flat tires for the entire unit. I was given directions to the tire yard and soon was scanning an area filled with rims, tires, and inner tubes. I didn't see Caddy anywhere.

I noticed a large steel tank about six feet by six feet and two feet deep. The box, which was filled with filthy water, was used to check flat tires to determine the location of the leaks. There was an air hose draped over the side of the tank and very few bubbles coming out of the hose, so I decided to kink the hose to see what would happen. Sure enough up came Caddy out of the muddy water, fully clothed and with the end of the hose in his mouth. He was wet and dirty, but he was getting some rest in the only pool for miles around.

Caddy gave me a big bear hug, and we exchanged the usual, "What have you been doing?" then decided that we would go get a beer together. Caddy walked into the office of the same petty officer I had just met and asked for the rest of the day off. The chief's response was, "Sure, as soon as you change the flat tires on those earth movers out on the lot."

We went outside and saw flats on two huge earthmoving pans with tires that were at least six feet tall. Normally it would take more than three hours to change a tire that big, since the earth movers would have to be jacked up and the wheels removed and broken down before the tire could be repaired. Then the process would have to be repeated in reverse order to get the vehicle moving again. But Caddy had a better idea.

Caddy instructed me to get a big forklift while he got a smaller one. I drove my forklift to the back of the earth-mover and lifted. The weight of the huge machine almost flattened the tires on my forklift, but Caddy was already driving his to the wheel where he loosened the lugs. He bumped it, and the big wheel fell off with a bang. A new tire was already made up and slung into place with a turn of an oversized lug wrench. The job was completed. Repairing the tire on the second earthmover went even faster, and the tires were changed in less than an hour. We left the tire yard and had our beer that afternoon.

I spent the next day with Caddy in the tire repair shop, swinging short handled sledge hammers, banging rims off flat tires. We worked very hard, but the change of scenery and the companionship of a good friend made it all worthwhile.

The Tire Yard

The Mint Green Truck

In the village of Thu Duc, our thirteen-man Seabee team worked with local officials to help build infrastructure that years of war had completely broken down. We hired locals and "taught" them building trades that they could use for employment after they graduated from our training program. The whole program was a farce in view of the fact that most of our workers already had skills far beyond our training knowledge.

We built small maternity hospitals, schools, bridges, roads, and community centers. We also built drainage systems to help keep villages from being washed away during the monsoon season.

As our work load progressed, we needed another truck to haul materials and crew members to job sites. Our supply system was nonexistent as we were far out in the countryside. Paul Wharen was our "procurement officer" and was always on the prowl looking for a bargain.

One afternoon Paul drove up in a two-and-a-half-ton United States Army truck. He had "acquired" the truck at a local army outpost many miles away. Now, Mr. Wharen was very efficient as he had also "acquired" a case of paint so that we could paint the truck to hide its identity. We all went to work that evening stripping away all the army identification markings and cleaning the truck in preparation for painting.

One of the mechanics, Jim Yost, was slightly upset when he found that there were only two colors of paint in the case, white and army green. If the identity of the truck was to be changed, the only choice was to mix the two colors together which we did. We painted our "new" truck a lovely mint green.

There was a contest to come up with the appropriate markings so that our new vehicle would look official. The winning design was a peace sign, which was prevalent at that time, incorporated with some normally seen logos. For some unknown reason, the truck was dubbed "the roach coach," although none of us smoked marijuana.

Our truck became known far and wide by the locals in all the surrounding villages and towns. I sometimes thought I was in a parade because we got so many waves when we drove down the dusty roads of South Vietnam. When traveling to jobs, the work crews all wanted to ride in the mint green truck because the attention that the truck drew made them feel like local celebrities.

We even took the truck to the army post to get fuel with no concern and never thought much about how some poor army PFC had explained losing a whole truck.

Lou and the Mint Green Truck

Lou on Bulldozer Clearing Jungle

Washed-out Road

Possessed in Phuoc Thinh

The narrow road that connected the small village of Phuoc Thinh to a larger dirt road had a huge washed out area caused by the heavy rains in the region. This posed a major obstacle in getting food and essential goods in and out of the village.

My work crew was assigned to survey the area and do what we could to repair the road. We were able to obtain large culverts to build a bridge over the washed out place.

Many of the young children in the village were captivated at seeing a large white man in their midst. The children would surround me and feel the hair on the backs of my arms. They kept getting in my way at work and were often so close that I would sometimes accidently step on their bare toes. When that happened, I would have to stop and comfort them.

One afternoon, J. C. Tanner came up in a dump truck with a large culvert chained to the back. I got an idea that I thought might solve the problem of having so many kids underfoot. After discussing the plan with J.C., we got busy with the implementation.

Now, J. C. was from South Carolina and, as a child, had gotten his two front teeth knocked out. Both teeth had been replaced by a bridge. J.C. stood in front of his dump truck, and I started making sounds and writhing about as if I were possessed. I pointed to J.C. with all my fingertips and screamed. J.C. loosened his bridge and fell back onto the bumper of the truck while pushing his front teeth out of his mouth with his tongue.

Then I turned to the crowd of children and started to scream and writhe in about the same way I had done toward J.C. The kids took the bait and scattered, covering their mouths with their hands.

I was not bothered again with a crowd of kids but did see them from a distance every day. When I would turn to look at them, they would put their hands over their mouths.

I began to feel bad about playing the joke on unsuspecting youngsters. They had never seen a bridge or false teeth before and were terrorized. I went to see one of the mothers and tried to explain that I was sorry but needed room to work. She seemed to understand.

The job took quite a long time, but the crowd of spectators kept their distance and allowed us to do our work.

Lou and J. C. Tanner

Barefoot Vietnamese Children Who Liked to
Watch the MCB 12801 Crew

Lou and Number One Laborer

International Bug Contest

During my second tour of duty, evenings were long and boring. After a long hard day of work in the hot Southeast Asia sun, we ate our meal and some of us would enjoy a cool beer or two. We never drank more than two for safety reasons: there were only thirteen of us, and we were far away from any other American soldiers.

There was time to write letters and not much else to entertain us. The armed forces radio was an option, but after seeing the war from both sides, we all now realized that the broadcasts were filled with propaganda.

One evening we decided to go outside to the mechanics shed for some fresh air. J.C. Tanner, Wharen, Mestayer, and I climbed on to the back of one of our trucks that was parked under a light in the mechanics shop.

We immediately noticed the grand variety of very unusual bugs that had assembled under the light. As we probed the bugs, we noticed that there were a couple that if turned on their backs would pop and flip in the air with a distinctive crack. The race was now on to try to catch some of these bugs so that we could have a contest to see whose bug could flip out of a ring drawn on the bed of the truck.

The captive bugs performed very well and soon the single ring was joined by several other rings that had various point values much like a dart board. We would predict and bet on how many rings each bug would clear. One at a time, we would place our bugs in the center of the ring and turn him over. He would pop as we cheered for him to reach one of the outside rings.

We had great entertainment for several weeks until the supply of the poppers seemed to disappear. There must have been some communication in the bug world about being captured and having to perform in the international bug flip contest.

Lou and Chris Mestayer

A Late Night Snack

For security, we all took turns walking the perimeter of our compound at night even though we knew we would be vastly outnumbered if the "bad guys" wanted us. We had a very small contingent of South Vietnamese soldiers who would man our two main bunkers, a total of four RVNs.

One night as I was making my round from bunker to bunker, I walked in on one of the South Vietnamese soldiers down on his hands and knees, retrieving a three-inch long cockroach. When he caught the critter, he held it by a hind leg while his comrade rolled up a sheet of paper and inserted the squirming roach into the tube. The soldier then set the paper on fire and toasted the roach.

After the roach was well done, the soldier tossed the crispy critter into his mouth and seemed to enjoy his snack. He then turned to me and asked me if I wanted one. He knew there were plenty around and that he would have no problem catching another. I declined his offer and got myself some instant mashed potatoes.

The Late Night Snack Bunker

A Visit from the Colonel

We were told that a high ranking colonel would be coming to see our camp on Sunday, and we needed to get ready. Our commanding officer, Lt. Tway, was in Saigon and would not be home in time for the visit so we were on our own. J.C. Tanner and I decided that we would give the colonel a good reception by being the standard country bumpkins and giving him a hearty welcome. We loaded up with large amounts of chewing tobacco and cigars.

Sure enough when Sunday came, a Huey circled our camp and finally landed in a field just north of our position. J.C. and I ran to the aircraft that was as shiny as a new one and waited to greet our guest. The colonel emerged in a nicely starched uniform and spit-shined shoes that defined a non-worker.

When the colonel approached, we extended our hands for a shake instead of a salute. As the colonel reflexively extended his hand, we immediately saluted. The colonel was off balance already, but before he could react we offered him a cheap cigar and said, "Welcome, Colonel." Then both of us spat out tobacco at the same time, J.C. to his right and I to my left.

We continued to work on the colonel who became somewhat uncomfortable with our lack of military bearing, but since there was no officer in charge, he had little choice but to ride along with us. The colonel only stayed for about twenty minutes during which J.C. and I kept telling him what we were doing in the area. J.C. would talk, and before the colonel could respond I would change the subject. When the colonel boarded his Huey and took off, we stood and waved, knowing that he would not be back to bother us again.

J.C. Tanner and Lou

Without Defense

Because we had orders to test fire our weapons, our policy was to do this every other Sunday in an open area a few miles from our camp. After a long period of being badgered, we were all in a sullen mood, so we decided to take out our frustrations during weapons testing. We fired our M60 machine guns until the barrel got so hot we lit cigars on the glowing steel. Then we launched M79 grenades until we got tired.

Upon return to base one of our newest members asked if he could clean the guns, and we all gladly agreed. Two weeks later when it was again time to test fire our weapons, the M60 would only fire one shot at a time. We took the guns apart and found that our new member had placed both recoil pistons in one gun. One gun had two pistons and did not have enough clearance to cock the next round in the chamber, and the other had no piston that would cock the gun at all.

For two weeks we had been without a defensive weapon and had not been aware of it. Needless to say, from that time forward, two of us cleaned the guns as a check and balance.

Machine Gun Practice

A Group from 128 Practices with Weapons

The Night Caller

I was working with a crew, building a road and a bridge in the village of Phouc Thinh. The road was about a mile long, and the bridge that had been there had washed out from the monsoon rains. The villagers were unable to get their crops out of the village, so we were asked to assist them.

I was driving a bull dozer, filling dirt onto the road bed, when the village chief came to ask if I could help him clear the jungle around his village for protection from the VC. I agreed and started to push the jungle back.

I was having fun clearing dense brush and trees when all of a sudden the ground gave way and the dozer dropped down about five feet. I immediately took the machine out of gear. The jarring impact had nearly knocked me out, and the air was so filled with dirt that it caused me to lose my bearing for a while.

I had caused a cave in from a tunnel of some sort and was now stuck. We used a large truck and some shovels to get the dozer out of the hole and were able to start clearing again in a few hours.

As I began pushing over a tree, a very large lizard fell on to the front hood of the dozer. The engine was extremely hot so I pushed the lizard off onto the ground and stopped the dozer. The animal was so stunned that I was able to catch him. I placed him in a spare sand bag to take back to our camp for a show and tell later that night.

That evening after we ate, I went out to my truck and retrieved the lizard to show the rest of the team. I planned to turn him loose the next day.

That night about 2:00 a.m., we were all awakened by a faint high pitched voice saying, "Fuck you, fuck you." Everyone was convinced that we were about to be over run, so we grabbed our weapons and helmets and crawled to the doors.

We positioned ourselves in a large circle to form a perimeter for defense. We kept hearing the voice "Fuck you, fuck you" so we slowly crawled toward the sound. It turned out that the lizard was making the sound. He was calling out in the middle of the night. Needless to say, I was not the most popular show and tell person in the camp for a few days after that event.

The week progressed, and I finished clearing the jungle from around the village. The night after I finished clearing, we were kept up with small arms fire into our camp. There was no doubt the bad guys did not appreciate us doing defensive perimeter work for the village.

We got the message loud and clear and told our Vietnamese workers the next day that we had made a mistake and would not do that again. We somehow knew that information would get to the right people.

Bombed in Phuoc Thinh

While I was working on the bridge at Phuoc Thinh, Caddy had a few days off, so he came down to visit me from where he was stationed in Quang Tri in the northern part of South Vietnam. Early one morning, I took him out to the job site to show him what we were doing.

As we were checking things out, an old woman came running up to our truck, crying and talking extremely fast. I had seen her several times before and knew she had a small farm in the area.

I calmed her down the best I could, and Caddy and I followed her as she motioned and lead the way to her farm where she had some animals, her only worldly possessions. As we approached, she pointed to an unexploded mortar in the ground just in front of her fence.

An unexploded mortar is extremely unstable, and we didn't know what to do. Then, Caddy suggested that we dig it up and move it. We carefully excavated the mortar and loaded it into our truck by holding one of the fins.

We rode about two miles down a dirty road where there was a large pit that had been formed from our digging to get dirt to use on the road. I lay on my stomach and threw the mortar over the edge. As soon as it hit the bottom, it detonated.

We went back to the little lady to let her know that everything would be okay. It was only then that we fully realized what a dangerous thing we had just done.

The lady and her animals were safe, and so were we. We had done our good deed for the day, maybe our good deed for several days.

Lou with the Mortar Lady

The Schoolhouse Grew

I was assigned a job to take my work crew of Vietnamese to build an addition to the local school in our village of Thu Duc. I consulted with Paul Wharen, one of my team members who helped acquire building materials, and we drew up plans in accordance with the materials we could obtain locally.

Our plans had the roof pitch too flat for my liking as it would be hot in the classrooms, but we had to use the building materials that were available. I started construction by making blocks of sand and cement and packing them in wooden forms to dry in the sun. Once dried, the blocks were delicate, but when stacked and covered with a layer of cement facing, they became strong enough to withstand the elements.

School was in session so I had the opportunity to interact with the children of the village. I truly enjoyed my interaction with the kids and even tried to play soccer with them during recess. They had a problem and kept telling me to take my boots off, as they were afraid I would kick them. They were all in bare feet and ran like little deer. I could not keep up so my playing time was limited.

One day, one of the older kids came and asked me if I would teach the English class. Their teacher had been assassinated the week before for obvious reasons. I agreed and was given a small book with a Vietnamese and English story. I do not remember the story as I was a little nervous. When the class began, there were about twelve children of various ages, but each time I looked up from the book, there were more faces staring at me. By the end of class, there were at least fifty children in the room. I never heard them come in. They just appeared.

I worked hard on the addition to make sure it was just right, and the children really seemed to enjoy my contact with them. On the final day of construction we had a dedication. The entire student body assembled in neat rows in the schoolyard, where I was thanked and presented about sixty handkerchiefs that had been embroidered by the female students in the school. I was moved to tears, as some were as exquisite as any New York high-end store could offer. Some were obviously a struggle for small hands and were equally as precious.

I took the handkerchiefs back to the camp and shared them with all of my team members. On my return to Gulfport, three days after hurricane Camille, my bags were lost so I never had the opportunity to see the gifts again, but the amazing experience still lasts in my memory.

Building a School

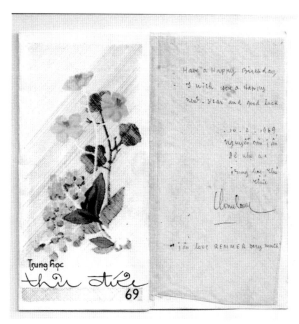

Birthday Card from Students to Lou

Thuduc highschool,

Dear Sir,

"Tet" will comes again on our country - with that happyness, I would like to send you many best wishes for new year . O.K ? Thanks a lot of your helps to build our school . And especially for your teaching me English .

I understand your kind . hearts when you work in the hot sun day by day or describe the difficult words by mouth, hands or eyes ... etc ...etc, I will remember all of these , forever .

You know , I have 2 aunts in the America now, so I know really that they are missing Vietnam very much . Some cases of you and all of . the U S soldiers . Am I correct ?

well, I wants to say again my wishes " Happy Newyear "to you . Please send my wishes to your friends , too . And thankyou very much for help me .

Affectionately,

Thuy .

Jan 29th, 1969 .

P.S : This is a spring card of my school .

Card of Thanks from Students to Lou

194

The Long Trip Home

At the end of my second deployment in August 1969, our group was taken to Saigon and housed in a rundown hotel. We were all very uneasy about spending the night there because we were worried about security. Even though our jungle home was far out in the country, we felt as though the enemy knew us and let us alone because we were working on THEIR bridges, schools, and communities.

After a fidgety night, we were taken to the airport and were boarded on what appeared to be an old C54 Skymaster, an aircraft left over from World War ll. The paint on the outside said "US NAVY," but all the markings on the inside told us it was really a timeworn Air Force plane. The aircraft had four piston engines, a tricycle landing gear, and windows covered with wire mesh. There were some regular seats and then jump seats near the rear where our gear was stowed.

When the plane was loaded and fired up, the noise was almost unbearable. We vibrated down the runway and lifted off on a prayer. We were free, but our feelings about leaving Vietnam were tempered with the thought that we had a long way to go in an antique aircraft.

First, we flew to Okinawa where we landed for fuel and a bathroom break. Near our plane, was parked a two-star general's staff car guarded by a marine corporal who was easily distracted long enough for us to place SEABEE stickers on each hubcap and, of course, on the bumper.

We left Okinawa and flew to Japan where we stayed for a few days. While there, we took the train to Tokyo and roamed the town, stopping for beer and gazing in amazement at all of the lights. After months in darkness in the woods, it was quite different to see the city with its hustle and bustle.

As we were gawking at our surroundings, we were approached by a short Japanese man who asked us if we wanted to have fun. We knew what he meant and said "Okay." The man guided us down an alley, over a fence, up a fire escape, through an open window, and into a room with a makeshift bar and several booths.

He left us there, where soon some unsavory ladies came into the room and started asking us if we wanted fun. We told the women we were having fun, and they seemed shocked at that response. The women persisted, and we dug in more saying that our companions were all that we needed. They retreated to another room and came back with other approaches, but we shunned all their advances. We had a great time turning the tables on these business women, and they were obviously stunned by the encounter.

Our flight left early the next day. The old plane flew so low that it seemed the Pacific Ocean was just under our wheels. The vibration and noise from the antiquated aircraft numbed us all over. Suddenly the plane started to descend towards the ocean, and as we looked through the grid of the windows, a small patch of sand appeared. The wheels of the landing gear seemed to nearly touch the waves before finding the runway. The brakes were applied, the engines were revved up, and we slowed until one wing seemed to stretch out over the ocean at the end of the runway. We had landed on Midway Island.

On Midway, we had breakfast and looked around. The island was hot, sunny, and very small. It was surprising how deserted the area was and how little infrastructure was near the airstrip. We took off later that afternoon and flew into the darkness.

Hours passed before we landed again, this time in Hawaii. We were exhausted by the constant noise and vibration of the plane. One of our crew knew a chief petty officer stationed in Hawaii, so the officer opened the Enlisted Men's club on base and treated us to steaks and free beer. When we finally got ready to board, he sent several cases of beer to our plane. The beer was loaded, and we prepared to take off. However, we didn't take off but were all escorted off the plane rather abruptly. Later, we found one of the engines had caught fire. After a half-day delay, we were on the plane again and off to the mainland.

While in the air, we started to drink the warm beer and, at least, act like we were having fun. A young flight crew member came back to our area and started to yell at us that it was illegal to drink on a military aircraft. One of our crew, a six-foot-two, imposing young man, stood up and told the young crewmember that we were going to drink or he would learn how to fly. The crewmember turned on his heels, and we never saw him again for the remainder of our trip.

We landed late at night in Oakland, California. I was finally back in the world! I called my sister, who was living in California, and told her to notify the rest of my family.

We left California in the morning and headed for Gulfport, Mississippi. Three days earlier, Hurricane Camille had hit the area, but we had no idea that such an event had devastated the Mississippi Gulf Coast since we had been stuck in the long route from our jungle home.

The trip from Oakland to Gulfport was supposed to take us to a joyous reunion with familiar and safe landscape. When we flew over Gulfport, we were shocked by what we saw. The pilot continued to fly to Mobile, then circled back and landed at Gulfport where we were unceremoniously dumped on the tarmac, and the plane flew away. The eerie silence of the place was unreal with the only sounds being those of buzzing chain saws. No birds could be seen, and the stillness was haunting.

It was several hours before a big truck came to take us to what was left of the base. Once there, we were told that there were no barracks, and we needed to leave and come back in two weeks for discharge. Some of our team were sent to Pensacola, Florida, for further assignment, and the rest of us were left to fend for ourselves.

I walked out of the South Gate to the nearby hospital where I had worked on my first stay in Gulfport. I knew there would be phone service there.

Caddy had come back two weeks earlier, and I knew he was still in the area. He had a girlfriend who lived north of Gulfport so I called her in order to get in touch with Caddy.

Caddy told me that he had a place to stay in Wiggins, Mississippi, a small town about twenty-five miles or so north of Gulfport. He invited me to join him there, and I readily accepted.

Caddy's place to stay turned out to be an empty, abandoned farm house in the woods. The house belonged to some of his girlfriend's family. The windows were gone, and the doors broken. I found two lawn chairs that became my bed. Since I had been an electrician in the Navy, I was able to tap into power from a pole that was located nearby and hook up electricity to the house. The house just happened to have an electric hot water heater, so we were able to bathe.

There was a coffee pot with no cord, but I improvised and got it working by using the cord from a broken lamp. The pot provided us with a way to boil water. We stayed in the house for two weeks, eating rice, instant potatoes, and grilled meats.

The 1960 Chevrolet Corviar that had been given to me by one of my fellow Seabees before I had left for my second tour provided transportation. Linda, the girl I had seen on the balcony and invited to go swimming, lived in the area and had kept it for me while I was gone. Unfortunately, Camille had blown out the back window.

The little Corvair smoked terribly and leaked oil. When it was driven fast, the vacuum created by the lack of a back window pulled smoke through the defrost system and gave the inside of the car a fine, blue coating of oil. When we stopped to gas up, we had to clean both the inside and outside of the front windshield in order to see.

I was finally discharged two weeks later, and Caddy and I decided to drive to Boston. Before we left on our journey, we got a GI can and went around to the gas stations that were still open and begged for the drain oil that was left from changing oil in customers' cars. The oil was like black tar but would serve us well for the long trip.

We took turns driving and when the smoke got too bad in the car we would take turns sitting on the rear shelf through the back window and lean on the roof. The fresh air was a delight even though we were going sixty miles an hour. Every time we stopped for gas we would pour up a quart mayonnaise jar full of the old oil and fill the crank case, and it worked just fine.

Caddy lost the keys so we had to hot wire the car to make it run, and we used a screwdriver to open the "trunk" which was in the front of Corvairs.

Our trip north went well until we entered the New Jersey Turnpike. We had only gone about five miles when we noticed a new white Oldsmobile Toronado following us. Soon we were stopped by the white car and we discovered that it was driven by a state trooper. The trooper just wanted to check us out since we were both wearing tank goggles and bandanas over our faces to protect ourselves from the oil that was coming in through the defrost system.

The officer wanted to search our car so we produced the screw driver and opened the trunk while offering an explanation. When it was opened, the officer spotted Caddy's rifle, and we were informed that we had to take it apart and scatter it in various parts of the car.

After a thorough search, the officer called his dispatcher to see if we were in compliance with all applicable laws, and was told we were. He decided that we were just a couple of nuts, so he told us we could go.

We tried to leave but soon discovered that our battery was dead and the car would not start. We needed a push to get on our way.

I got out of the car and asked the trooper if he would give us a push, and he readily agreed. Once we got up to speed, Caddy popped the clutch, and the car coughed back to life.

I looked in the rear view mirror and saw the new unmarked car covered in dark blue smoke with oil splatter over the front. The trooper had started his window washers so I told Caddy to speed up. We kept going and never looked back. We drove the entire turnpike and were stopped again at the north end with a less grueling interrogation.

We arrived in Saugus, Massachusetts, late in the evening and parked the car in the front yard of Caddy's mother's house.

We played in Boston for a few days and then I boarded a bus and returned to Delaware where my family lived. I had intended to go to the University of Delaware but was not accepted. It seemed that I could risk my life in Vietnam, but I was not good enough to attend the University of Delaware.

It was still a long, long way home.

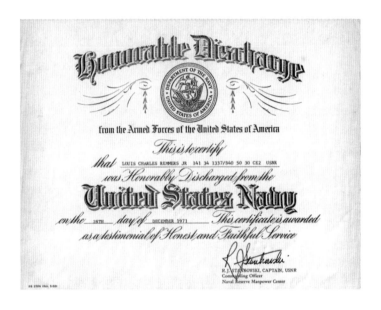

Home and Pregnant

I had just gotten home from the war in Vietnam and felt numb all over. While I was away my parents had moved to Newark, Delaware, where I knew only one person, a girl I had dated while we were living in New Jersey, who was attending the University of Delaware.

I called her on the wild hunch that she might want to go to a movie with me. She didn't accept my movie offer but invited me to come to a Halloween party at her dorm. She said we could have a good time.

I made the mistake of telling my mother about the invitation, and she, sensing that I was depressed and stressed, decided to do something to cheer me up. She called the next-door neighbor and together they helped me get "dressed" for the party. I was not particularly up for a "Trick or Treat" party but decided to let Mom help me feel better.

Mom and the neighbor opted to fix me up as a pregnant woman. I put on hose, makeup, and a dress with appropriate padding and was sent off to the party after a much-to-long fashion show.

Louis Remmers

When I arrived at the dorm, there was already a crowd of young people in all sorts of garb. The dorm had two housing units that were connected by a common social area.

I buzzed my "date" and went into the common area thinking I would watch her try to pick me out of the crowd. As I was waiting, I attracted quite a lot of attention with more and more kids coming by trying to guess who was behind the mask. No one had any idea that not one of them knew me.

I spied my date walking down the hall from her housing unit with her real date, and I was left alone with all of those curious college kids who were now starting to tease me. Those poor kids didn't know what had recently happened to me and my fellow service men and women. They were on a free ride having fun, knowing little about tragedy and the reality of life and death. I took off my mask, and everyone was surprised that I was a stranger.

I got up and left the party, but it was too early to go home to face Mom and the neighbor. I didn't want to give an account of the night's activities. Still dressed as a pregnant woman, I went to Stone Balloon Bar and had several beers, hoping that a desperate drunk would not try to pick me up.

I finally went home and told Mom that I had a great time and might want to go to the University of Delaware for school. That never happened.

Reflexes and Reflections

In 1966, I would come home from work, and the news on television would be showing the carnage of the Vietnam War. For the first time in the history of our country, the horrors of war were displayed to the noncombatants in our country.

Did the display harden the public to the horrors of war or was that reserved for the mothers and fathers of those who were serving? I found out soon enough that the war was real, and the numbers and names on the nightly news actually represented lives and families and communities across America.

The psychology of the war was not lost on anyone who served in Vietnam. Initially, when first arriving in country, everyone was in a state of shock. All the training and preparation could not prepare a young man for the fact that this was the real thing. The games were over. The whistle had blown. Real blood was being shed.

For the first three months or so, the rookie soldier would be extremely apprehensive and afraid of his own shadow. I can remember lying in bed thinking of what I would do if a mortar round hit the roof of the hooch. My plan was to roll to the right and get under my bunk in order to shield myself from the slaughter. These unrealistic thoughts prevailed among all of us because some of my fellow soldiers wore helmets and flak jackets to bed.

Our daily activities were also tainted with constant fear. Which one of the work trucks would be blown up today? If we stopped in a village, would a woman or a child roll a hand grenade under our feet?

After about three months the newness wore off, and total fatigue set in. We no longer cared. What would happen would happen, and that was that. There was no longer enough energy to be afraid. Everyone focused on the job at hand and worked hard, taking one day at a time.

As the months rolled by, we became "short," and it was time to again be frightened. We were getting ready to go back into the world, and we did not want to waste our lives by getting killed after enduring Vietnam for all those months. The anxiety and fear became more intense as we waited for the clock to tick down and finally signal the time to go home.

The days were filled with painful teasing as we watched the huge transport planes flying out taking troops back to the world. The giant planes would bank toward the South China Sea and disappear over the horizon and off to freedom.

The anticipation of home helped us tolerate the conditions in Nam. We were going to go home, get a car, and hang out with our friends one more time just to let ourselves know we were real. Life would again be normal.

Thoughts of going home were a constant motivation, and the memories of home were larger than life.

When we arrived back in the world, things had changed. All those days of dreaming about how it would be were fantasy. Friends had changed, and we had changed. We no longer fit in. We were no longer boys, or even young men, but people who had lived through a very difficult experience and were not appreciated by our fellow countrymen.

Many of the atrocities we had seen and experienced were not things to share with family or friends. Coming home was like returning to another planet. We were now seeing new style cars and clothing and advances in technology that were made for life and not for death and destruction. The fabric of society had become silk, and we were all threads of burlap.

The training of the military and our experiences followed us and remained a constant in our lives. There was no switch to turn off and stop what we had learned and seen. One night during a severe thunderstorm in Delaware, I found myself in the front yard looking for my foxhole. I woke myself up yelling, "Take cover."

Another time, I was driving my dad's car on Broad Street in my own home town of Philadelphia when a car back-fired, and I found myself parked in the median lying on the floorboard.

Reflexes are difficult to turn off, especially when they are initiated by fear. I can still identify Huey choppers and C130 transport planes by the sounds they make. I smell the gunpowder at the Fourth of July fireworks display and am taken back to a place far away.

I do not know how many tears were shed by the World War II veterans, but I know that when they were alone or when the lights were out, they were transported back to their war. How much courage they displayed to not reveal the secrets that haunted them.

I once read an article quoting the answers that a veteran had given a reporter during an interview. The reporter asked, "Have you ever had nightmares about the war?" To that the veteran responded, "Yes." The reporter followed up by asking, "When?" to which the veteran responded, "Last night."

When was there never a war? Nation's leaders find ways to destroy without getting the blood of their young men on their own hands. Only veterans can truly appreciate what war means. There is always a sense of sadness. We still question, "Why did it happen?"

Epilogue

After Vietnam, I bounced around a lot. I went to Delaware where my parents had moved while I was in the service and felt lost because I didn't know anyone. I went to church regularly with my parents but found that I had to fight to keep from crying each Sunday. The pain was too much, so I decided to go back to Gulfport, Mississippi.

I drove twenty-six straight hours in a Volkswagen Karman Ghia and stayed with my future wife and her roommate. I looked for work and never even realized the destruction caused by Hurricane Camille.

I became a day laborer, which is one of the most depressing things a young man can do. All the dreams of coming back to the "world" that sustained us all in Vietnam suddenly vanished. The world had changed and left us all behind, and even though our expectations were to take up just where we left off when we went off to war, we had changed. Life is like that.

I waited around the employment office in Gulfport and jumped in the back of pickup trucks that came to the office to find day workers. I worked in many areas, mostly hard labor. My fellow workers were the saddest people I had ever encountered with no hope or aspirations to be better. They worked just enough to buy beer or wine then they were gone.

I finally landed a permanent job building sidewalks for a construction company. I worked with two black men who were much older and who constantly complained that I was working too hard and too fast. My hard work made them look bad, and I believe they knew I was supposed to be doing something better with my life. I worked for several weeks and then decided to return to Delaware.

I got a job with the State of Delaware driving a big track bulldozer in the swamps around the Delaware River. I worked through the winter and finally moved back to Jackson, Mississippi, and married my Gulfport girlfriend.

In the early days, I worked for UPS and then for Sally Beauty Company selling beauty supplies to beauty shops all over Central Mississippi. I finally took a few courses at Hinds Community College and then transferred to the University of Southern Mississippi.

I was very frustrated most of the time because even though I had experienced life and death situations in Vietnam, I was now doing what amounted to busy work. The students and I could not relate very well because I was already twenty-five years old, and most of them were nineteen or twenty. That age difference was not very great, but it was worlds apart after all I had experienced.

I had to work harder than most of the students, but I was dedicated and knew I needed to get an education. The dream of education seemed somewhat hollow, but the kinds of work I had been doing were not making me feel as though I was getting anywhere. I was lost and trying to find my identity.

I was the student who ate at the cafeteria and was very happy with the quality of the food available. The kids there had never had to eat survival rations or food that was considered not fit for human consumption.

I worked hard in class and was seen as a geek who was not really a geek. I knew the kids were trying their best to figure me out. Some of the students kept their distance because they knew I was a veteran and had heard that the Vietnam vet could "snap" at any moment.

Late one afternoon as I was walking to the library, I found myself walking behind three Vietnamese students who had been in the military of Vietnam. I was listening to their conversation when I thought how strange it was that I could actually understand what they were saying, and they did not realize that anyone besides themselves knew what was being said.

College is a place to learn and grow, but I felt as if I had already grown far beyond my expectations while still being pressured by the system to follow the yellow brick road and complete the initiation before progressing to the next step.

I did not apply for my diploma at USM even though I had enough credits. I applied to the Physical Therapy program at the University Medical Center in Jackson and was accepted. It would be six months before classes started at the medical center, so I worked those six months running a chicken hatchery for Marshal Durbin Farms.

I really dug into my job and took care of my illiterate workers. I showed them I cared about them, and they took care of me. We hatched two hundred fifty thousand chickens each week. My crew was the least educated in society and for the most part cast offs. I treated them with respect and helped them whenever I could, and our productivity went off the charts.

Before I left to go to physical therapy school, the CEO of Marshal Durbin flew in from Birmingham, Alabama, to offer me a job with his "team" because he realized that the output of my hatchery was greater than all the company's other facilities without increased costs. This increase in productivity happened because as the hatchery equipment wore out, I went to the processing plant's workshop and fabricated the parts needed to keep the operation running. Working in a chicken hatchery was an adventure to say the least.

I had to move on with my plans to be a physical therapist. My workers were saddened when I left, and, on my last day at the hatchery, they all gathered with tears in their eyes to wish me well. I knew they were better off because someone had finally showed them respect which gave them some dignity. I can only hope that they were able to carry that with them.

As the saying goes, hindsight is 20/20. The experience of Vietnam had many a varied impact on those of us who experienced it. It made me a better person. I can always say a bad day is not too bad because no one is shooting at me.

The very concept of one person trying to kill another whom he does not know is insane to me. I cannot imagine how one can justify random killing. I experienced the impact of war on all angles: From the bitter sadness of a family around a dining room table, to the wounded soldiers, to the widows in Vietnam who never had closure in the loss of a husband or brother. There have been so many who have shed tears that betrayed their "John Wayne" inspiration. So many have been hardened, and lives have been changed forever by that tragedy.

I wish I could have done more for those who needed help. I did help the Vietnamese people on my second tour and was greeted with warm loving thanks. I especially enjoyed the children who were innocent and free to give love and respect.

The horrors of war keep one off balance for years after the service. Getting used to the possibility of being killed at any moment weighs heavily on each individual. After surviving by thinking of how we would resume our lives back in the "world," we returned only to find that was all a fantasy.

We returned from war to a world that had changed and never missed us, and in fact, did not want us in the conscious reality of being present in that world. Day-to-day life had continued as usual, and we were not a part of it. There was hostility in many quarters, but in others, there was just total disregard.

It is very easy for one to return to the nightmares of war if one does not keep busy and keep things in perspective. The old saying, "Good steel cannot be made without a lot of heat" could apply. In order to be hard and able to withstand the pressures of life you must be able to look at the experience from every angle.

My thoughts and prayers are always with my comrades who made that hard journey. Many of the mothers and fathers who suffered the bitter burden of loss are no longer with us, and in a way are relieved of their sorrow.

I do find it ironic that our grand government does not see the errors of its ways and still deems it necessary to send good young men, and now women, off to sacrifice for no clear cut reason.

Vietnam War Statistics

There are 58,267 names now listed on that polished black wall, including those added in 2010.

The names are arranged in the order in which they were taken from us by date, and within each date the names are alphabetized.

Beginning at the apex on panel 1E and going out to the end of the East wall, appearing to recede into the earth (numbered 70E - May 25, 1968), then resuming at the end of the West wall, as the wall emerges from the earth (numbered 70W - continuing May 25, 1968) and ending with a date in 1975. Thus the war's beginning and end meet. The war is complete, coming full circle, yet broken by the earth that bounds the angle's open side and contained within the earth itself.

The first known casualty was Richard B. Fitzgibbon, of North Weymouth, Massachusetts, listed by the U.S. Department of Defense as having been killed on June 8, 1956. His name is listed on the Wall with that of his son, Marine Corps Lance Cpl. Richard B. Fitzgibbon III, who was killed on Sept. 7, 1965.

Louis Remmers

There are three sets of fathers and sons on the Wall.

A total of 39,996 on the Wall were just 22 or younger.

The largest age group, 8,283 were just 19 years old.

Some 3,103 were 18 years old.

Twelve soldiers on the Wall were 17 years old.

Five soldiers on the Wall were 16 years old.

One soldier, PFC Dan Bullock was 15 years old.

Some 997 soldiers were killed on their first day in Vietnam.

Some 1,448 soldiers were killed on their last day in Vietnam.

Thirty-one sets of brothers are on the Wall.

Thirty-one sets of parents lost two of their sons.

Fifty-four soldiers on the Wall attended Thomas Edison High School in Philadelphia.

Eight women are on the Wall. They were nursing the wounded.

A total of 244 soldiers were awarded the Medal of Honor during the Vietnam War; 153 of them are on the Wall. Beallsville, Ohio, with a population of 475, lost six of her sons.

West Virginia had the highest casualty rate per capita in the nation. There are 711 West Virginians on the Wall.

The Marines of Morenci: They led some of the scrappiest high school football and basketball teams that the little Arizona copper town of Morenci (pop. 5,058) had ever known and cheered. They enjoyed roaring beer busts. In quieter moments, they rode horses along the Coronado Trail, stalked deer in the Apache National Forest. In the patriotic camaraderie typical of Morenci's mining families, the nine graduates of Morenci High enlisted as a group in the Marine Corps. Their service began on Independence Day, 1966. Only 3 returned home.

The Buddies of Midvale: LeRoy Tafoya, Jimmy Martinez, Tom Gonzales were all boyhood friends and lived on three consecutive streets in Midvale, Utah on Fifth, Sixth and Seventh avenues. They lived only a few yards apart. They played ball at the adjacent sandlot ball field. And they all went to Vietnam. In a span of 16 dark days in late 1967, all three would be killed. LeRoy was killed on Wednesday, Nov. 22, the fourth anniversary of John F. Kennedy's assassination. Jimmy died less than 24 hours later on Thanksgiving Day. Tom was shot dead assaulting the enemy on Dec. 7, Pearl Harbor Remembrance Day.

The most casualty deaths for a single day was on January 31, 1968 ~ 245 deaths.

The most casualty deaths for a single month was May 1968 ~ 2,415 casualties were incurred.

Seabees

Who are the Seabees?

Seabees are members of the United States Navy construction battalions. The word Seabee is a proper noun that comes from the initials of Construction Battalion, (CB) of the United States Navy. The Seabees have a history of building bases, bulldozing, and paving thousands of miles of roadway and airstrips, and accomplishing a myriad of other construction projects in a wide variety of military theaters dating back to World War II.

What was the role of the Seabees during the Vietnam War?

Seabees were deployed to Vietnam throughout the conflict beginning in small numbers in June 1954 and extending to November 1972. By 1962, they began building camps for Special Forces. In June 1965, Construction Mechanic 3rd Class Marvin G. Shields, part of Seabee Team 1104, was actively engaged at the Battle of Dong Xoai and was posthumously awarded the Medal of Honor for his actions there. Shields remains the only Seabee ever to be awarded the Medal of Honor. These "Civic Action Teams" continued into the Vietnam War where Seabees, often fending off enemy forces alongside their Marine and Army counterparts, also built schools and infrastructure and provided health care service. Beginning in 1965, full Seabee battalions (MCBs) and Naval Construction Regiments (NCRs), along with other unit types, were deployed throughout Vietnam. Seabees from the Naval Reserve provided individual personnel early on to augment regular units and two battalions, MCB 12 and MCB 22.

In Vietnam, the Seabees supported the Marines and built a staggering number of aircraft-support facilities, roads, and bridges; they also paved roads that provided access to farms and markets, supplied fresh water to countless numbers of Vietnamese through hundreds of Seabee-dug wells, provided medical treatment to thousands of villagers, and built schools, hospitals, utilities systems, roads, and other community facilities. Seabees also worked with and taught construction skills to the Vietnamese people. — *Wikipedia*

Maternity Hospital Built
by the Thirteen-man Team MCB 12801

About the Author

After Vietnam, Lou had several jobs: A day laborer in Gulfport, building sidewalks in Biloxi, driving a bulldozer to help with mosquito control along the river in the swamps of Delaware. He tried technical school in Delaware, and then moved back to Mississippi where he married. He took two classes at Hinds County Community College in Raymond, Mississippi, and then transferred to The University of Southern Mississippi before attending Physical Therapy School at the University of Mississippi Medical Center in Jackson.

While Lou was still attending school, he and his wife, Linda, were blessed with the birth of two wonderful daughters, Kimberly and Stacy. After graduation, he took a job in Corinth, Mississippi, where he worked for eight years before moving to Alexandria, Louisiana, for three years.

In 1986, Lou moved to Tupelo, Mississippi, and opened the first free standing private practice for Physical Therapy in north Mississippi. Lou calls himself semi-retired and continues to see patients three days a week in Tupelo. At last count, his chart numbers were over 28,000 patients seen while in private practice in Tupelo. Lou says, "I continue to learn and grow as a practitioner and love what I do. I continually find new ways to help achieve my goals of helping people achieve function and reduce pain in their lives." His patients agree.

Recently, Lou was listening to a motivational CD entitled "Change Your Thoughts, Change Your Life" by Dr. Wayne Dyer. Lou knows that his thoughts and his life were forever changed by his experiences in Vietnam. The following is paraphrased from Dr. Dyer's CD and adapted by Lou to express his thoughts about war and his experiences in Vietnam:

Weapons are tools of ill omen wielded by the ignorant. If their use is unavoidable, the wise act with restraint. The greatest sorrow is to be a veteran and to witness the atrocities of humanity. When you hold a real weapon, you will feel its character strongly. It begs to be used. It is fearsome. Its only purpose is death and destruction. Its power is not just in the material of which it is made, but the intention of its maker.

It is regrettable that sometimes weapons must be used, but on occasion, survival demands it. The wise go forth only as a last resort. They never rejoice in the skill of the weapon, nor do they glorify war.

When death, pain, and destruction visit that which is held sacred, the spiritual price is devastating. A greater hurt than one's own suffering is witnessing the suffering and death of others. The revulsion of seeing human beings act their worst and the sheer pain of not being able to help their victims can never be erased.

When you go personally to war, you cross the line yourself. You sacrifice ideals for survival, and the fury of killing alters you forever. That was why very few rushed to serve in the military.

Being led to war by thinking you are doing what is right, blinds one to the truth of the unalterable change. Think before you want to change unalterably. The stakes are not merely one's life but one's very humanity.

How much energy in the world has been used to build things that are destined to destroy others? Every victory in war should be treated as a funeral; there are no winners. All war is the absence of being with the creator. It is estimated that over one hundred million lives were lost in the last century because of war.

Louis Remmers

Rice Truck by Day, Funeral Hearse by Night

The End